JOURNEY INTO NARNIA

JOURNEY INTO NARNIA

by Kathryn Lindskoog

HOPE PUBLISHING HOUSE
Pasadena, California

For information address:

Hope Publishing House
P.O. Box 60008
Pasadena, CA 91116 – U.S.A.
Tel: 626-792-6123 / Fax: 626-792-2121
E-mail: hopepub@loop.com
Web site: http://www.hope-pub.com

Cover and text design — Greg Endries Design
Cover artist — Tim Kirk
Interior illustrators — Tim Kirk & Patrick Wynne

Printed in the U.S.A. on acid-free paper

Library of Congress Cataloging-in-Publication Data

Lindskoog, Kathryn Ann.
    Journey into Narnia / by Kathryn Lindskoog.
        p.   cm.
    Includes bibliographical references and illustrations.
    ISBN 0-932727-89-1
    I. Lewis, C. S. (Clive Staples), 1898–1963. Chronicles of Narnia.
2. Children's stories, English — History and criticism. 3. Fantastic
fiction, English — History and criticism. 4. Christian fiction, English
— History and criticism. I. Title
PR6023.E926C5354 1997
823'.912 — dc21   97-18312
                                                 CIP

To Jonathan and Jennifer,
Peter and Kathleen

C.S. LEWIS'S RESPONSE TO THIS BOOK

Magdalene College,
Cambridge
Oct 29th 1957

"[*The Lion of Judah in Never-Never Land*] arrived yesterday and I read it at once. You are in the center of the target everywhere. For one thing, you know my work better than anyone I've met, certainly better than I do myself. (I've no recollection whatever of *The World's Last Night* and can't imagine what it was about!) But secondly you (alone of the critics I've met) realize the connection or even the unity of all the books—scholarly, fantastic, theological—and make me appear a single author not a man who impersonates half a dozen authors which is what I seem to most. This wins very high marks indeed. . . .

With thanks and good wishes,

Yours sincerely

C.S. Lewis

CONTENTS

PREFACE

This book consists of two parts. Part One, *The Lion of Judah in Never-Never Land: The Theology of C.S. Lewis Expressed in His Fantasies for Children,* was completed in 1957. C.S. Lewis read it then and heartily approved. When first published, in 1973, it was commended by Edmund Fuller in the Wall Street Journal: "An excellent exposition of the sinewy theology that underlies the Narnia tales."

Part Two, *Exploring the Narnian Chronicles,* takes the seven books in chronological order and discovers the heart of each one, with an abundance of fresh new background information and Biblical parallels. These concise insights and applications are designed for personal reading pleasure as well as practical helps for teachers, parents and ministers.

Narnia expertise should never become an end in itself. C.S. Lewis fell in love with Norse mythology when he was an adolescent, and because it gave him a very special kind of joy he studied it on his own. "I could have passed a pretty stiff examination on my subject," he recalled. "And I went on adding detail to detail, progressing toward the moment when I should know most and should least enjoy." Eventually the joy was gone.

So it is that studying Narnia too hard would be a mistake. Noticing ever more about Narnia should be like peeking into closets, setting out to sea or longing for Aslan's country. That's how Lewis would want it.

The joy of dwelling mentally in Narnia is only a vivid reminder. It is a reminder of the most important and joyful things there are.

FOREWORD

C.S. Lewis As Children's Author

The *Iliad* is great because all of life is a battle;
the *Odyssey* is great because all of life is a journey.

—G.K. Chesterton

C.S. Lewis never tired of rereading the *Iliad* and the *Odyssey*. One reason the Narnian Chronicles are great is that like the *Iliad* and the *Odyssey* they are about life's battle and life's journey.

Homer wrote the *Iliad* and the *Odyssey* in Greek about the time of the first Olympics, circa 800 B.C. Next, Virgil wrote an epic titled the *Aeneid* in Latin circa 20 B.C. and intentionally echoed Homer. (Some of the very earliest Christians probably read at least part of Virgil's *Aeneid*, because it was extremely popular in Rome in the days of Christ and his followers.)

Dante wrote the first Christian epic, *The Divine Comedy*, in ordinary Italian in about A.D. 1300. Then in 1660 Milton wrote the second great Christian epic in English, *Paradise Lost*. (Lewis knew and loved both of these.) All five epics—The *Iliad* and *The Odyssey, The Aeneid, The Divine Comedy* and *Paradise Lost*—were works of genius that have delighted multitudes of readers.

Lewis's first career ambition was to publish book-length story-poems like those, with grand themes, lofty language and bits of humor.

Incredible as it seems, throughout the 2,500-year span from 800 B.C. to A.D. 1660, when our five great epics were produced, there was no such thing as a children's book. There were no children's writers at all. People told stories to children, but no one wrote a storybook for them to enjoy until 250 years ago. Books for children came along like an afterthought in the book world.

Books for children also came along like an afterthought in the writing career of C.S. Lewis. He had always loved children's stories, and in middle age he suddenly started writing them. It is interesting to see how he included key elements of the great epics in his books for children: grand themes, voyages or struggles with profound consequences, and immensities of cosmic history.

In other ways Lewis's overwhelming success as a writer of children's books resembles the story of Charles Dodgson, better known as Lewis Carroll. (Lewis Carroll published *Alice's Adventures in Wonderland* in 1865.) Both C.S. Lewis and Lewis Carroll were brilliant Oxford professors who had no children of their own. Both of them were devoutly Christian and much concerned with ultimate realities as well as with ethics and character. Both were full of fun. Both wrote about people tumbling or stumbling into another world. And both meant for their children's stories to be read by adults just as much as children.

PART ONE

THE LION OF JUDAH
IN NEVER-NEVER LAND

The Theology of C.S. Lewis
Expressed in His Fantasies for Children

. . . though I thought not of thee under the form of a human body, yet was I constrained to image thee to be something corporeal in space, either infused into the world, or infinitely diffused beyond it . . . since whatsoever I conceived, deprived of this space, appeared as nothing to me, yea, altogether nothing, not even a void. . . .

—St. Augustine, *The Confessions*

These things which are said of God and other things are predicted neither unequivocally nor equivocally, but analogically. . . . Accordingly, since we arrive at the knowledge of God from other things, the reality of the names predicated of God and other things is first in God according to his mode, but the meaning of the name is on him afterwards. Wherefore he is said to be named from his effects.

—St. Thomas Aquinas, *Summa contra Gentiles*

As to Aslan's other name, well, I want you to guess. Has there never been anyone in this world who (1) Arrived at the same time as Father Christmas; (2) Said he was the Son of the Great Emperor; (3) Gave himself up for someone else's fault to be jeered at and killed by wicked people; (4) Came to life again; (5) Is sometimes spoken of as a Lamb (at the end of the "Dawn Treader")? Don't you really know his name in this world?

—C.S. Lewis, a letter to an American girl

CHAPTER ONE

MAKING PICTURES

Images of God

"To forbid the making of pictures about God would be to forbid thinking about God at all, for man is so made that he has no way to think except in pictures." Thus Dorothy Sayers states the premise underlying the pictorial symbolism used by C.S. Lewis in his delightful series of children's books, *The Chronicles of Narnia*. She continues with the broader assertion that all language about everything is analogical and that we think in a series of metaphors. We can explain nothing in terms of itself, but only in terms of other things.[1]

Lewis himself, in his book *Miracles*, refutes attempts to conceive of God without the use of metaphorical images:

> "I don't believe in a personal God", says one, "but I do believe in a great spiritual force." What he has not noticed is that the word "force" has let in all sorts of images about winds and tides and electricity and gravitation. "I don't believe in a personal God", says another "but I do believe we

---

[1] *The Mind of the Maker* (New York: Harcourt, Brace, 1941), p. 22.

are all parts of one great Being which moves and works through us all"—not noticing that he has merely exchanged the image of a fatherly and royal-looking man for the image of some widely extended gas or fluid. A girl I knew was brought up by "higher thinking" parents to regard God as a perfect "substance"; in later life she realized that this had actually led her to think of him as something like a vast tapioca pudding. (To make matters worse, she disliked tapioca.) We may feel ourselves quite safe from this degree of absurdity, but we are mistaken. If a man watches his own mind, I believe he will find that what profess to be specially advanced or philosophic conceptions of God are, in his thinking always accompanied by vague images which, if inspected, would turn out to be even more absurd than the man-like images aroused by Christian theology."[2]

But the Christian doctrine of God is not the only concept embodied in the Narnian tales. Lewis has subtly and intricately woven into them a variety of Christian doctrines—though of course religious concepts are secondary to Lewis's first concern, a rollicking good story. Readers are more than welcome to miss the Christian teaching—at least on the conscious level.

The doctrines fall into three main categories: Lewis's concept of nature—the system of all phenomena in space and time; Lewis's concept of God—the creator, redeemer and sustainer of nature and humankind; and Lewis's concept of humans in their relationship to nature, God and their fellow humans. The basis of these concepts is neither fundamentalism nor modernism, but Lewis's particular Christian orthodoxy, which Chad Walsh has termed Classical Christianity.[3]

---

[2] New York: Macmillan, 1947, pp. 90–91.

[3] *C.S. Lewis, Apostle to Skeptics* (New York: Macmillan, 1949), p. 171.

Lewis's Childhood Writing

Before seeking out Lewis's Christian beliefs in his books for children, one might consider the nature of these fantasies. Lewis claimed to write the kind of books he himself liked to read. Hence it is not surprising that his stories for children contain the subject matter that interested him as a child.

His early literary tastes are clearly recalled in the autobiographical story of his conversion, *Surprised by Joy*. Here he tells us that he had soon staked out a claim to one of the attics and made it his "study." It was in this little retreat that his first stories were written and illustrated, with enormous satisfaction. They were an attempt to combine his two chief literary pleasures, "dressed animals" and courtly "knights-in-armour." As early as his sixth, seventh and eighth years, the mood of the systematizer was already strong in him. This led from romancing to historiography—he set about writing a full history of "Animal-Land," complete with a map and colorful illustrations created from his paint box.[4]

Lewis's continued regard for geography is apparent in his Narnian series, as well as in his literary criticism. Of William Morris's romances he once said, "Other stories have only scenery; his have geography."[5] That evaluation can be applied to his own stories as well.

Although the fairy tales he wrote as an adult contain the same emphasis upon knights in armor, history and geography as characterized his youthful efforts, Lewis is quick to emphasize the major difference between the two. Of the former, he depreciatively comments: "My invented world was full (for me) of interest, bustle, humour and character; but there was no poetry, even no romance in it. It was almost astonishingly prosaic." He notes: "For readers of my children's books, the best way of putting this would be to say that Animal-Land had nothing whatever in common with Narnia except

---

[4] *Surprised by Joy* (London: Geoffrey Bles, 1955), pp. 19–20.
[5] Charles A. Brady, "Introduction to Lewis," *America*, June 10, 1944. p. 269.

the anthropomorphic beasts. Animal-Land, by its whole quality, excluded the least hint of wonder."[6]

As a child, Lewis had not yet acquired the Christian Romanticism[7] which motivates his Narnian tales and distinguishes them from the earlier fantasies. The Narnian tales seem to illustrate the assertion of J.R.R. Tolkien that "the Gospels contain a fairy-story, or a story of a larger kind which embraces all the essence of fairy-stories." The Gospels "contain many marvels—peculiarly artistic, beautiful and moving: 'mythical' in their perfect, self-contained significance; and at the same time powerfully symbolic and allegorical; and among the marvels is the greatest and most complete conceivable eucatastrophe," the Birth of Christ. "The Resurrection is the eucatastrophe of the story of the Incarnation."[8]

According to Tolkien,

> there is no tale ever told that men would rather find was true and none which so many skeptical men have accepted as true on its own merits. . . . To reject it leads either to sadness or to wrath. It is not difficult to imagine the peculiar excite-ment and joy that one would feel if any specially beautiful fairy story were found to be 'primarily' true, its narrative to be history, without thereby necessarily losing the mythical or allegorical significance that it had possessed. . . . The Christian joy, the *Gloria*, is of the same kind. . . ."[9]

---

[6] *Surprised by Joy*, p. 22.

[7] In describing Charles Williams as a Christian romantic, Lewis states: "A romantic theologian does not mean one who is romantic about theology but one who is theological about romance, one who considers the theological implications of those experiences which are called romantic. The belief that the most serious and ecstatic experiences either of human love or of imaginative literature have such theological implications, and that they can be healthy and fruitful only if the implications are diligently thought out and severely lived, is the principle of all his work"—"Preface," *Essays Present-ed to Charles Williams*, ed. C.S. Lewis (Grand Rapids, Michigan: Eerdmans, 1966), p. vi.

[8] "On Fairy Stories," *Essays Presented to Charles Williams*, p. 83.

[9] "On Fairy Stories," pp. 83–84.

Although the child Lewis was not yet acquainted with these concepts, he had experienced that undefinable desire, that romantic longing, referred to by German poets as *Sehnsucht*. This is obvious in the imaginative preoccupations of his childhood: "I wish I had time to tell you of all the other constructions—the unknown room in the house which one was always hoping to discover, the chess men coming alive as in *Alice*, the garden which was partly in the West and partly in the past. . . ." [10]

The Narnian Series

These very elements of subject are present in the Narnian Chronicles; along with richly romantic settings and details. Lewis defends this literary mode with a commentary on the contrasting approach of T.S. Eliot:

> Mr. Eliot may succeed in persuading the reading youth of England to have done with robes of purple and pavements of marble. But he will not therefore find them walking in sackcloth on floors of mud—he will only find them in smart, ugly suits walking on rubberoid. It has all been tried before. The older Puritans took away the maypoles and the mince-pies, but they did not bring in the millennium, they only brought in the Restoration. If Mr. Eliot disdains the eagles and trumpets of epic poetry because the fashion of this world passes away, I honour him. But if he goes on to draw the conclusion that all poetry should have the penitential qualities of his own best work, I believe he is mistaken. As long as we live in merry middle earth it is necessary to have middle things. [11]

---

10 C.S. Lewis, "Psychoanalysis and Literary Criticism," *Essays and Studies*, XXVII (1942), 18.
11 *A Preface to Paradise Lost* (London: Oxford, 1942), p. 133.

In accordance with this position, Lewis's children's books employ both the trumpets and eagles of epic poetry and simple merriment. They glorify such epic scenes as "that wonderful hall with the ivory roof and the west door all hung with peacock's feathers and the eastern door which opens right onto the sea"[12] and also idealize the more "middle" domesticities such as taking tea in a clean little cave. "And really it was a wonderful tea. There was a nice brown egg, lightly boiled, for each of them and then sardines on toast. . . ."[13]

Whether grand or trivial, every scene in the Narnian series is colored by *Faërie*. According to Tolkien, "Faërie . . . may perhaps most nearly be translated by Magic—but is magic of a peculiar mood and power, at the furthest pole from the vulgar devices of the laborious, scientific magician." [14] Indeed, this type of magician is thoroughly ridiculed by Lewis in *The Magician's Nephew*. Lewis's Faërie, agreeing with Tolkien's definition,[15] "contains many things besides elves and fays and besides dwarfs, witches, trolls, giants, or dragons: it holds the seas, the sun, the moon, the sky; and the earth and all things that are in it: tree and bird, water and stone, wine and bread and ourselves, mortal men, when we are enchanted." The heart of the desire of Faërie is fantasy, the making or glimpsing of Other-worlds.[16]

According to G.K. Chesterton, whom Lewis credits as greatly clarifying Christianity for him,[17] "The only right way of telling a story is to begin at the beginning—at the beginning of the world. Therefore all books have to be begun in the wrong way for the sake of brevity." [18]

Lewis's story begins in his first published Narnian book at the time when London children were evacuated to the country during the Sec-

---

[12] C.S. Lewis, *The Lion, the Witch and the Wardrobe* (New York: Macmillan, 1950), p. 148.

[13] *Ibid.*, p. 11.

[14] "On Fairy Stories," p. 43.

[15] *Ibid.*, p. 42.

[16] *Ibid.*, p. 63.

[17] *Surprised by Joy*, p. 210.

[18] G.K. Chesterton, *William Blake* (London: Duckworth, 1910), p. 1.

ond World War. The four Pevensie children, boarding at a country estate, find their way through an old wardrobe into the land of Narnia. Their adventures there lead into three other books of the same scheme, that of children from this world transported by magic into a world of fairy-tale creatures belonging to a great lion. The fifth book published is the tale of two native children of that world who also are chosen by the great Lion to serve the land of Narnia and to know him in a special way.

Only in the sixth book published does Lewis begin at the beginning—at the beginning of the world of Narnia. The intrusion of two Victorian children into that newborn world begins the complications which give rise to all the later adventures. In the seventh and last book of the series these events are culminated in the end of the world of Narnia.[19]

Each of these adventures, although complete in itself, opens doors to many other possible accounts of episodes in the history of Narnia. Each is written in the tone of George MacDonald[20] at the conclusion of his book *The Princess and the Goblin:*

> "—But there! I don't mean to go any farther at present."
> "Then you're leaving the story unfinished, Mr. Author!"
> "Not more unfinished than a story ought to be, I hope.
> If you ever know a story finished, all I can say is I never did.

---

19 Thus the chronological order of the books by events is as follows:

The Magician's Nephew (1955)

The Lion, the Witch and the Wardrobe (1950)

The Horse and His Boy (1954)

Prince Caspian (1951)

The Voyage of the "Dawn Treader" (1952)

The Silver Chair (1953)

The Last Battle (1956)

20 "I regarded him as my master; indeed I fancy I have never written a book in which I did not quote from him"—C.S. Lewis, *George MacDonald* (New York: Macmillan, 1954), p. 20.

21 New York: Macmillan, 1926, p. 267.

Somehow stories won't finish. I think I know why, but I won't say that either, now." [21]

Tolkien refers to George MacDonald in his analysis of types of fairy stories, stating that fairy stories as a whole have three faces: "the Mystical towards the Supernatural; the Magical towards Nature; and the Mirror of scorn and pity towards Man." Of course, the essential face of Faërie is the Magical one. If the others appear at all, the degree is variable and may be decided by the individual storyteller. "The Magical, the fairy-story, may be used as a *Miroir de l'Homme*; and it may (but not so easily) be made a vehicle of Mystery. This at least is what George MacDonald attempted." [22]

Apparently C.S. Lewis has followed MacDonald's example. As seen in the résumé of his fairy stories, this series is fragmentary. Yet each book is a vehicle of mystery. There is a strong unity of philosophy and consistency of doctrine throughout the collection of whimsical episodes—Lewis's concepts of nature, of God and of human life.

---

21 New York: Macmillan, 1926, p. 267.
22 "On Fairy Stories," p. 53.

CHAPTER TWO

SPOILED GOODNESS: LEWIS'S CONCEPT OF NATURE

Rural Beauty

Lewis's appreciation of geographical landscape is what one would expect of a Christian romantic—a reverent and insatiable delight. In his personal account, he relates:

> What the real garden had failed to do, the toy garden did. It made me aware of nature—not, indeed, as a storehouse of forms and colours but as something cool, dewy, fresh, exuberant. . . . As long as I live my imagination of Paradise will retain something of my brother's toy garden.[1]

Lewis's wonder at the fresh exuberance of nature is expressed in his first description of the real Narnia, as the great thaw occurs in *The Lion, the Witch and the Wardrobe*. The sudden rejuvenation of the forest is recorded with great delicacy and sensuous detail. Finally, as the trees

---

[1] *Surprised by Joy*, p. 14.

11

begin to come alive, the larches and birches in green, the laburnums in gold, a dwarf stops and announces with horror, "This is no thaw; this is spring"(pp. 97–98).

In contrast to this poignant presentation of nature approached with childlike eagerness is Lewis's short story "The Shoddy Lands," an adult fantasy. The shoddy lands are discovered upon an accidental journey into the mind of a frivolous young woman. There the scenery is extremely vague and dingy, each nondescript feature of the surrounding merely a crude, shabby apology for part of nature. There is no freshness, detail or clarity, because the woman's mind is jaded and blasé.[2]

Again, at the opposite extreme, the rich profuseness of nature is sensuously exaggerated in Lewis's description of the Wood between the Worlds in *The Magician's Nephew:*

> You could almost feel the trees growing. . . . a pool every few yards as far as his eyes could reach. You could almost feel the trees drinking the water up with their roots. This wood was very much alive. . . . It was a *rich* place: as rich as plum-cake.[3]

Here Lewis is apparently reverting to "the older conception of Nature . . . tingling with anthropomorphic life, dancing, ceremonial, a festival not a machine."[4] In an early poem, Lewis once said,

> Faëries must be in the woods
> Or the satyrs' laughing broods—
> Tritons in the summer sea,
> Else how could the dead things be
> Half so lovely as they are? . . .[5]

---

[2] "The Shoddy Lands," *The Best from Fantasy and Science Fiction: Sixth Series* (New York: Doubleday, 1957), p. 159.

[3] New York: Macmillan, 1955, pp. 25–26.

[4] C.S. Lewis, *English Literature in the Sixteenth Century* (Oxford: Clarendon, 1954), p. 4. For Lewis's scholarly analysis of the history and uses of the word nature, read "Nature" in his book *Studies in Words* (London: Cambridge, 1960), pp. 24–74.

[5] Clive Hamilton [C.S. Lewis], "Song," *Spirits in Bondage* (London: William Heinemann, 1919), p. 73.

Later, Lewis developed this idea in lively prose in his introduction to D.E. Harding's *The Hierarchy of Heaven and Earth*. "We have emptied the baby out with the bath," he states. "In emptying out the dryads and the gods (which, admittedly, 'would not do' just as they stood) we appear to have thrown out the whole universe, ourselves included."[6] According to Lewis, a dryad is the abbreviated symbol for all we know about trees. So is "mind or consciousness" a symbol for what we know about behavior. Rejection of these concepts occurs when the symbol is mistaken for the object.[7]

> At the outset the universe appears packed with will, intelligence, life and positive qualities; every tree is a nymph and every planet a god. Humans themselves are akin to the gods. The advance of knowledge gradually empties this rich and genial universe first of its gods, then of its colours, smells, sounds and tastes, finally of solidity itself as solidity was originally imagined. As those items are taken from the world, they are transferred to the subjective side of the account classified as our sensations, thoughts, images or emotions. The Subject becomes gorged, inflated, at the expense of the Object. But the matter does not rest there. The same method which has emptied the world now proceeds to empty ourselves. The masters of the method soon announce that we were just as mistaken (and in much the same way) when we attributed "souls" or "selves" or "minds" to human organisms, as when we attributed Dryads to the trees. Animism apparently begins at home. We, who have personified all other things, turn out to be ourselves mere personifications.[8]

The structure of Lewis's children's books is in direct opposition to the philosophy decried in this introduction.

---

[6] New York: Harper, 1952, p. 12.

[7] *Ibid.*, p. 12.

[8] *Ibid.*, p. 10.

The Supernatural

The Narnian series hinges upon the acceptance of supernatural phenomena:

> "Supposing I told you I'd been in a place where animals can talk and where there are—er—enchantments and dragons—and—well, all the sorts of things you have in fairy tales." Scrubb felt terribly awkward as he said this and got red in the face.
>
> "How did you get there?" said Jill. She also felt curiously shy.
>
> "The only way you can—by Magic," said Eustace almost in a whisper.[9]

There are, of course, skeptics in these books. In *The Lion, the Witch and the Wardrobe* the children did not accept Lucy's tale about discovering Narnia when they first heard it. They consulted the wise old professor about her strange story. They complained that when they looked in the wardrobe there was nothing there, asserting that if things are real they're there all the time. "Are they?" the Professor said. The time element also bothered the children. During less than one minute, Lucy claimed to have spent several hours in Narnia. "That is the very thing that makes her story so likely to be true," said the Professor. He explained that if there really was a door in his house that led to some other world, it would be very likely that the other world had a separate time of its own so that however long one stayed there it would never take up any time on earth.

"But do you really mean, Sir," asked one of the boys, "that there could be other worlds—all over the place, just round the corner—like that?" (pp. 39–40).

When the children had had actual experiences with the supernatural, the concept of other worlds was much easier to accept. Once

---

[9] *The Silver Chair* (New York: Macmillan, 1953), p. 4.

they had been out of their own world, they could conceive of many others with comparative facility. The idea came to Digory in *The Magician's Nephew*: "Why, if we can get back to our own world by jumping into *this* pool, mightn't we get somewhere else by jumping into one of the others? Supposing there was a world at the bottom of every pool!" (p. 30).

The philosophy underlying this structure of multiple natures is clearly explained in a speculative passage in *Miracles* (p. 20). Lewis begins with the supernaturalist's belief that a Primary Thing exists independently and has produced our composition of space, time and connected events which we call nature. There might be other natures so created which we don't know about. Lewis is not referring here to other solar systems or galaxies existing far away in our own system of space and time, because those would be a part of our nature in spite of their distance. Only if other natures were not spatiotemporal at all or if their space and time had no relation to our own, could we call them different natures. This is important in Lewis's literary theory:

> No merely physical strangeness or merely spatial distance will realize that idea of otherness which is what we are always trying to grasp in a story about voyaging through space: you must go into another dimension. To construct plausible and moving "other worlds" you must draw on the only real "other world" we know, that of the spirit.[10]

The only relationship to our system would be through common derivation from a single supernatural force. Here Lewis resorts to the figure of authorship discussed by Dorothy Sayers in *The Mind of the Maker*.[11] The only relationship between events in one novel and events in another is the fact that they were written by the same author, which causes a continuity in the author's mind only.

------

[10] "On Stories," *Essays Presented to Charles Williams*, p. 98.
[11] *Miracles.* p. 118.

There could be no connection between the events in one nature and the events in another, by virtue of the character of the two systems. But perhaps God would choose to bring the two natures into partial contact at some point. This would not turn the two natures into one, because they would still lack the total reciprocity of one nature, and this spasmodic interlocking would arise, not from within them, but from a divine act. Thus, each of the two natures would be "supernatural" to the other. But in an even more absolute sense, their contact itself would be supernatural, because it would be not only outside of a particular nature but beyond any and every nature.[12]

When this philosophical speculation is geared to a childhood level of interests, delightful possibilities for story situations appear. One of these, the concept of our world being known elsewhere as a myth, is introduced by the prince of Narnia to his young English guest:

> "Do you mean to say," asked Caspian, "that you three come from a round world (round like a ball) and you've never told me! It's really too bad of you. Because we have fairy-tales in which there are round worlds and I always loved them. I never believed there were any real ones. But I've always wished there were and I've always longed to live in one. Oh, I'd give anything—I wonder why you can get into our world and we never get into yours? If only I had the chance! It must be exciting to live on a thing like a ball. Have you ever been to the parts where people walk about upside down?"
>
> Edmund shook his head. "And it isn't like that," he added. "There's nothing particularly exciting about a round world when you're there."[13]

Just as our world bears aspects of a fairy-tale world from the Narnian point of view, so the Narnian world is rich with figures of earthly folklore. For example, there are giants, both good and bad. But they

---

[12] *Ibid.*, p. 21.

[13] *The Voyage of the "Dawn Treader"* (New York: Macmillan, 1952), p. 195.

affect us in much the same way. "A *good* giant is legitimate: but he would be twenty tons of living, earth-shaking oxymoron. The intolerable pressure, the sense of something older, wilder and more earthy than humanity, would still cleave to him." [14]

In Narnia, giants, centaurs, dryads, fauns, dwarfs, sea serpents, mermaids, dragons, monopods and pirates live in an environment of castles, caves, magic whistles, golden chessmen and enchanted gardens. The implication is that all elements of myth as we know them are shadows of a foreign reality. This idea is also demonstrated in Lewis's science fiction trilogy. [15]

The Corruption of Nature

C.S. Lewis is known for opposing the spirit of modern thought with the unpopular Christian doctrines of sin and evil. He considers evil not as a nebulous abstraction but as a destructive immanence which should be openly recognized and not complacently ignored, even though such recognition is disquieting. This principle is the major element in Lewis's otherwise happy concept of nature. [16] In his own words, "We find ourselves in a world of transporting pleasures, ravishing beauties and tantalizing possibilities, but all constantly being destroyed, all coming to nothing. Nature has all the air of a good thing spoiled." [17] In *The Magician's Nephew* original sin enters Narnia ". . . before the new, clean world I gave you is seven hours old, a force of evil has already entered it; waked and brought hither by this son of Adam" (p. 121).

Throughout the rest of the series, this element of evil manifests itself in Narnia in various forms, always subjugating and trying to destroy the goodness in nature. In *The Lion, the Witch and the Wardrobe* the leader of evil forces is the White Witch, who has banished spring:

---

[14] Lewis, "On Stories," p. 95.

[15] *Out of the Silent Planet* (1938), *Perelandra* (1943), *That Hideous Strength* (1945)

[16] Walsh, *C.S. Lewis, Apostle to Skeptics*, p. 81.

[17] *Miracles*, p. 147.

"... it is she that has got all Narnia under her thumb. It's she that makes it always winter. Always winter and never Christmas" (p. 14).

In *Prince Caspian* a wise old dwarf informs the Prince of the harm done by evil King Miraz, who has trampled out the natural beauty of Narnia. He assures the Prince that what he had heard about Old Narnia is true. "It is the country of Aslan, the country of the Waking Trees and Visible Naiads, of Fauns and Satyrs, of Dwarfs and Giants, of the gods and the Centaurs, of Talking Beasts"; but the wicked king no longer allows them to be spoken of.[18] This is the situation lamented by Lewis in an early lyric:

> The faërie people from our woods are gone,
> No Dryads have I found in all our trees.
> No Triton blows his horn about our seas
> And Arthur sleeps far hence in Avalon.[19]

In *The Silver Chair* another witch has assumed power, this time by suppression of the glad natural order of the world beneath the surface of the earth, reminiscent of Wagner's Nibelheim.[20] There she enchanted merry dwarfs from the deep land of Bism and brought them up near the surface of the earth to Shallowlands to work for her in a state of glum amnesia. She is planning a great invasion of Narnia. The idea of invasions and battles is basic to those books.

"Enemy-occupied territory—that is what this world is," Lewis plainly states in *Mere Christianity*.[21] Yet he consciously avoids slipping into dualism, which he defines as "the belief that there are two equal and independent powers at the back of everything, one of them good and the other bad and that this universe is the battlefield in which they fight out an endless War" (p. 33).

In *The Last Battle* the form of the evil power is roughly the shape

---

[18] *Prince Caspian* (New York: Macmillan, 1951), pp. 41–42.

[19] Hamilton [Lewis], "Victory," *Spirits in Bondage*, p. 16.

[20] Richard Wagner, *The Ring of the Nibelung* (New York: Garden City, 1939), p. 38.

[21] New York Macmillan, 1952, p. 36.

of a human, but it has the head of a bird of prey with a cruel, curved beak and long bird-like claws. It carries a deathly smell.[22] This creature closely resembles the old Priest of Ungit in *Till We Have Faces*, who looks like a dreadful vulture and bears the evil Ungit smell with him.[23]

"If evil has the same kind of reality as good, the same autonomy and completeness, our allegiance to good becomes the arbitrarily chosen loyalty of a partisan." [24] Lewis makes it clear in *The Lion, the Witch and the Wardrobe* that the power of evil is inferior to the power of good. The power of good is that of the great king:

> "He's the king. He's the Lord of the whole wood, but not often here, you understand. Never in my time or my father's time. But the word has reached us that he has come back. He is in Narnia at this moment. He'll settle the White Queen all right...."
>
> "She won't turn him into stone too?" said Edmund.
>
> "...Turn *him* into stone? If she can stand on her two feet and look him in the face it'll be the most she can do and more than I expect of her" (pp. 63–64).

The return of spring in this book is one of the many reflections of Norse mythology in the Narnian series. This source was one of the strongest influences upon Lewis's early years. In his long poem *Dymer* he writes:

> And from the distant corner of day's birth
> He heard clear trumpets blowing and bells ring,
> A noise of great good coming into earth
> And such a music as the dumb would sing
> If Balder had led back the blameless spring

---

[22] London: The Bodley Head, 1956, pp. 85–86.

[23] Grand Rapids, Michigan: Eerdmans, 1966, p. 54.

[24] "Evil and God," *Spectator*, CLXVI (February 7, 1941), 141.

With victory, with the voice of charging spears,
And in white lands long-lost Saturnian years.[25]

So it is that the return of summer brings inexpressible joy to Narnia and, the wintry witch having been defeated, "Summer is queen/ Summer is queen in all the happy land." [26]

Later on, the king himself explains to the children that "though the Witch knew the Deep Magic, there is a magic deeper still which she did not know." Her knowledge went back "only to the dawn of Time." [27]

The limitations of evil are discussed in *Mere Christianity*, where Lewis states, as he does in *The Screwtape Letters*, that wickedness is the pursuit of something good in the wrong way. One can be good for the sake of goodness even when it hurts, but one cannot be bad for the sake of badness. One is cruel for the pleasure or usefulness of it, not for the sake of cruelty itself. Badness cannot be bad in the way that goodness is good, for badness is only spoiled goodness (p. 35).

Spoiled goodness is illustrated in the beginning of sin in Narnia, as related in *The Magician's Nephew*. Digory had been sent to a distant garden to fetch a silver apple. On the gate was written this verse:

Come in by the gold gates or not at all,
Take of my fruit for others or forbear.
For those who steal or those who climb my wall
Shall find their heart's desire and find despair (p. 141).

Digory was just turning to go back to the gates when he stopped for one last look and received a terrible shock. There stood the Witch, throwing away the core of an apple which she had eaten. The juice had made a horrid dark stain around her mouth. Digory guessed that she must have climbed in over the wall. He began to see the truth in the last

---

[25] Clive Hamilton [C.S. Lewis], *Dymer* (New York: E.P. Dutton, 1926), p. 105.
[26] Lewis, "The Ocean Strand," *Spirits in Bondage*, p. 46.
[27] Lewis, *The Lion, the Witch and the Wardrobe*, p. 132.

line of the verse, because "the Witch looked stronger and prouder than ever . . . but her face was deadly white, white as salt" (pp. 141–44).

The king explained the result of this act to the children later. The Witch had fled from the garden to the North of the World, where she was growing stronger in dark Magic. She would not dare to return to Narnia so long as the tree was flourishing there, because its fragrance had become a horror to her. "That is what happens to those who pluck and eat fruits at the wrong time and in the wrong way," the king concluded. "The fruit is good, but they loathe it ever after" (p. 157).

The preponderance of dark magic and witches in Lewis's books gives the impression that he is greatly concerned with demonology. However, the overall tone of his work echoes the glad assurance of St. Paul, "For I am sure that neither death, nor life, nor angels, nor principalities, nor things present, nor things to come, nor powers, nor height, nor depth, nor anything else in all creation will be able to separate us from the love of God in Christ Jesus our Lord" (Rm 8:38).

In contrast to the everlasting quality of God's love, which is his principal message, Lewis reminds us that the physical world is in a process of disintegration. He seems to agree with the concept of Sir James Jeans, that "If the inanimate universe moves in the direction we suppose, biological evolution moves like a sailor who runs up the rigging in a sinking ship." [28]

In Lewis's opinion, the modern conception of progress, as popularly imagined, is simply a delusion, supported by no evidence. Darwinism gives no support to the belief that natural selection, working upon chance variations, has a general tendency to produce improvement. Lewis asserts that there is no general law of progress in biological history. He calls the idea of the world slowly ripening to perfection a myth, not a generalization from experience. He feels that this myth distracts us from our real duties and our real interests. [29]

---

[28] Sayers, *The Mind of the Maker*, p. 139.

[29] "The World's Last Night," *His*, XV (May, 1955), p. 4. Also available in *The World's Last Night and Other Essays* (New York: Harcourt, Brace, 1960), pp. 93–113.

This attitude is illustrated by the depressing picture of a dying world given in *The Magician's Nephew:*

> The wind that blew in their faces was cold, yet somehow stale. They were looking from a high terrace and there was a great landscape spread out below them. Low down and near the horizon hung a great, red sun, far bigger than our sun. Digory felt at once that it was also older than ours; a sun near the end of its life, weary of looking down upon that world. To the left of the sun and higher up, there was a single star, big and bright. Those were the only two things to be seen in the dark sky; they made a dismal group. And on the earth, in every direction, as far as the eye could reach, there spread a vast city in which there was no living thing to be seen. And all the temples, towers, palaces, pyramids and bridges cast long, disastrous-looking shadows in the light of that withered sun. Once a great river had flowed through the city, but the water had long since vanished and it was now only a wide ditch of grey dust.
>
> "Look well on that which no eyes will ever see again," said the Queen. "Such was Charn, that great city, the city of the king of kings, the wonder of the world, perhaps of all worlds" (pp. 52–53).

At "The End of This Story and the Beginning of all the Others," in the Wood between the Worlds (ch. 15, *The Magician's Nephew*), the children learned the fate of Charn and received a warning. They saw a little hollow in the grass, with a warm, dry bottom. Aslan told them that the hollow had been the pool that they had jumped into to go to the dying world of Charn. "There is no pool now. The world is ended, as if it had never been. Let the race of Adam and Eve take warning" (p. 159).

In *The Last Battle* Jill declares, "*Our* world is going to have an end some day. Perhaps this one won't . . . wouldn't it be lovely if Narnia just went on and on. . . ?"

"Nay," she was answered, "all worlds draw to an end; except Aslan's own country." Jill was just replying that she hoped that the end of Narnia was millions of years away, when news came that Narnia was overthrown, with this message from the lips of a dying friend: ". . . remember that all worlds draw to an end and that noble death is a treasure which no one is too poor to buy." [30]

The destruction of Narnia began with the invasion of commerce and the plunder of nature by greedy men. The idyllic forest was ruthlessly destroyed in a sacrilegious turmoil by crowds of imported workers, before the rightful owners realized what was happening. This is an exact parallel to the development of the near-fatal dangers in Lewis's adult book about Britain, *That Hideous Strength*.[31]

The actual end of Narnia was a dramatic pageant of mythical splendor. It concluded with the moon being sucked into the sun and the world freezing forever in total darkness. Here Lewis follows the tradition of the North rather than the conventional Christian concept of destruction by fire. Peter, High King of Narnia, was given the key to the door of heaven and locked out the cold.[32]

Lewis's response to nature, then, is threefold. First is romantic appreciation and idealization. Second is analysis leading to an acceptance of the supernatural and to speculation about it. Third is moral awareness of the force of evil in nature and of the temporal quality of our world. Each of these responses is basic to Lewis's Christian philosophy and is an important influence upon his books for children. Nature is more than a background setting for the action of his characters. "Either there is significance in the whole process of things as well as in human activity, or there is no significance in human activity itself." [33]

---

[30] *The Last Battle* (New York: Macmillan, 1956), pp. 92–95.

[31] *Ibid.*, pp. 26–27.

[32] *The Last Battle*, p. 159.

[33] C.S. Lewis, *The Personal Heresy* (London: Oxford, 1939), p. 29.

CHARN
by Tim Kirk

CHAPTER THREE

THE COMING OF THE LION: LEWIS'S CONCEPT OF GOD

"They say Aslan is on the move—perhaps has already landed."

And now a very curious thing happened. None of the children knew who Aslan was any more than you do; but the moment the Beaver had spoken these words everyone felt quite different. Perhaps it has sometimes happened to you in a dream that someone says something which you don't understand but in the dream it feels as if it had some enormous meaning—either a terrifying one which turns the whole dream into a nightmare or else a lovely meaning too lovely to put into words, which makes the dream so beautiful that you remember it all your life and are always wishing you could get into that dream again. It was like that now. At the name of Aslan each one of the children felt something jump in his inside.[1]

---

[1] Lewis, *The Lion, the Witch and the Wardrobe*, p. 54.

This passage is the first reference to Aslan in the Narnian Chronicles. Through the use of this character, who sprang into the story
unbidden, Lewis has expressed with disarming simplicity his many-
faceted concept of God. This is the same general concept of God that
St. Augustine attempted to describe without the aid of allegory:

> What art thou then, my God? . . . Most highest, most good,
> most potent, most omnipotent; most merciful, yet most
> Just; most hidden, yet most present; most beautiful, yet most
> strong; stable, yet incomprehensible; unchangeable, yet all-
> changing; never new, never old; all-renewing and bringing
> age upon the proud and they know it not; ever working, ever
> at rest; still gathering, yet nothing lacking; supporting, fill-
> ing and overspreading; creating, nourishing and maturing;
> seeking, yet having all things. Thou lovest, without passion;
> are jealous, without anxiety; repentest, yet grievest not; are
> angry, yet serene; changest thy works, thy purpose unchang-
> ed; receivest again what thou findest, yet didst never lose;
> never in need, yet rejoicing in gains; never covetous, yet exact-
> ing usury. Thou receivest over and above, that thou mayest
> owe; and who hath aught that is not thine?[2]

As Dorothy Sayers has emphasized in *The Mind of the Maker*, we seek
to interpret the nature of God by means of analogies drawn from our
own experience. One of our favorite analogies is that of a king. We
talk of God's kingdom, his laws and his dominion (p. 24). Aslan is a
king—yet one must remember that he is not a king in this world, but
in an animal land.

God's Bodily Form

"Aslan a man!" declares one of his subjects. "Certainly not. I tell
you he is the king of the wood and the son of the great Emperor-

---

[2] *The Confessions* I. iv.

Beyond-the-Sea. Don't you know who is King of Beasts? Aslan is a lion—*the* Lion, the great Lion." [3]

The use of a lion as a symbol of power is a Scriptural device. The book of Proverbs refers to "the lion, which is mightiest among beasts and does not turn back before any" (30:30, RSV). Earlier it compares the growling of a lion to the wrath of a king (20:2). The prophet Hosea goes one step further and likens the roaring of a lion to the wrath of God himself (11:10). Finally, in Revelation the lion is used as a specific symbol of Christ. St. John records, "Then one of the elders said to me, 'Weep not; lo, the Lion of the tribe of Judah, the Root of David, has conquered . . .' " (5:5, RSV).

But Lewis, though clearly influenced by the Bible, does not rely upon Scriptural justification for his imagery. The nature of Narnia demands it. Dorothy Sayers, in a capricious bit of speculation, has captured the gist of this necessity:

> There is, of course, no reason why an infinite Mind should not reveal itself in an infinite number of forms, each being subject to the nature of that particular form. It was said, sneeringly, by someone that if a clam could conceive of God, it would conceive of him in the shape of a great, big clam. Naturally. And if God has revealed himself to clams, it could be only under conditions of perfect clamhood, since any other manifestation would be wholly irrelevant to clam nature. By incarnation, the creator says in effect "See! this is what my eternal Idea looks like in terms of my own creation; this is my manhood, this is my clamhood, this is my characterhood in a volume of created characters." [4]

The scene in which the children first meet the eternal Idea in *The Lion, the Witch and the Wardrobe* is one of awe. They don't know what to do or say when they see him. People who have not been in Narnia

---

[3] *The Lion, the Witch and the Wardrobe*, p. 54.
[4] *The Mind of the Maker*, p. 90.

think sometimes that a thing cannot be good and terrible at the same time. If the children in this story had ever thought so, they were cured of it now. When they tried to look at Aslan's face, they just caught a glimpse of the golden mane and the great, royal, solemn, overwhelming eyes; and then they found that they couldn't look at him at all and "went all trembly" (p. 103).

In contrast to the faun-like God of Kenneth Grahame's *The Wind in the Willows*,[5] a book which Lewis enjoyed,[6] the God in Lewis's books is not semi-animal; God is super-animal. Such a super-animal is conceived of in *The Problem of Pain*:

> But if there is a rudimentary Leonine self, to that also God can give a "body" as it pleases him—a body no longer living by the destruction of the lamb, yet richly Leonine in the sense that it also expresses whatever energy and splendour and exulting power dwelled within the visible lion on this earth. . . . I think the lion, when he has ceased to be dangerous, will still be awful indeed, that we shall then first see that of which the present fangs and claws are a clumsy and satanically perverted, imitation. There will still be something like the shaking of a golden mane. . . .[7]

Lewis's description of Aslan seems to be based on the great archetypical lion in *The Place of the Lion*, by Lewis's friend Charles Williams:

> . . . the shape of a full grown and tremendous lion, its head flung back, its mouth open, its body quivering. It ceased to

---

[5] Kenneth Grahame also reveals God to children in a form suitable to the creatures in his story. In an extensive poetic passage, the enraptured Rat and Mole approach the Divine Presence. Mole raised his fearful eyes and saw the kind Friend and Helper; the graceful sweep of his horns, the hooked nose, the bearded smile, the strong arms and broad chest, the panpipes in his hand, and the shaggy limbs and hooves. "All this he saw, for one moment breathless and intense, vivid in the morning sky; and still, as he looked, he lived; and still, as he lived, he wondered"—Kenneth Grahame, *The Wind in the Willows* (New York: Scribner's, 1954), pp. 135–36.

[6] *Surprised by Joy*, p. 34.

[7] New York: Macmillan, 1948, pp. 130–31.

roar and gathered itself back into itself. It was a lion such as the young men had never seen in any zoo or menagerie; it was gigantic and seemed to their dazed senses to be growing larger every moment. Of their presence it appeared unconscious; awful and solitary it stood and did not at first so much as turn its head. Then majestically, it moved; it took up the slow forward pacing in the direction which the man had been following; it passed onward and while they stared it entered into the dark shade of the trees and was hidden from sight.[8]

The same impregnable, awesome stateliness was encountered by the first human beings to accidentally see Aslan at the beginning of Narnia in *The Magician's Nephew*. In reading this passage, one notes the similarity to Williams' account:

It was coming on, always singing, with a slow, heavy pace. . . . Though its soft pads made no noise, you could feel the earth shake beneath their weight. . . . The children could not move. They were not even quite sure that they wanted to. The Lion paid no attention to them. Its huge red mouth was open, but open in song not in a snarl. It passed by them so close that they could have touched its mane. They were terribly afraid it would turn and look at them, yet in some queer way they wished it would. But for all the notice it took of them they might just as well have been invisible and unsmellable. When it had passed them and gone a few paces further it turned, passed them again and continued its march eastward (pp. 95–96).

Aslan possesses the same twofold nature that Lewis, in his theological writings, attributes to Christ. It is the paradox of orthodox Christianity: Jesus was fully human and at the same time fully divine.

---

[8] Grand Rapids, Michigan: Eerdmans, pp. 14–15.

Lewis's commentary on this doctrine is an elaboration on the principle that everywhere the great enters the little. Its power to do so is almost the test of its greatness. Because he believes in the power of the Higher, just in so far as it is truly Higher, to come down, the power of the greater to include the less,[9] Lewis presents a God capable of becoming a true lion.

His thinking on this point developed in accordance with the teaching of G.K. Chesterton. As Chesterton expressed the principle:

> The more we know of higher things the more palpable and incarnate we shall find them. . . . Not till we know the high things shall we know how lowly they are. . . . Meanwhile, the modern superior transcendentalist will find the facts of eternity incredible because they are so solid; he will not recognize heaven because it is so like the earth.[10]

The true beasthood of Aslan is made clear in *The Horse and His Boy*. The horse Bree is smugly stating his sophisticated concept of Aslan's form to his friends. With alarm they watch an enormous lion, bigger and more yellow and beautiful and alarming than any other, approaching him from behind. Bree is just explaining that when people spoke of him as a Lion they meant only that he was as strong as a lion or as fierce as a lion. It would be absurd to suppose that he was a *real* lion. It would be disrespectful. If he was a lion he would have to be a Beast just like everyone else.

In revealing himself, Aslan urges the now frightened horse to test his bodily form "Do not dare not to dare. Touch me. Smell me. Here are my paws, here is my tail, these are my whiskers. I am a true Beast."[11] In the Gospel of John, Christ said to Thomas, "Put your finger here and see my hands; and put out your hand and place it in my side; do not be faithless, but believing" (20:27, RSV).

---

[9] *Miracles*, pp. 134–35.

[10] *William Blake*, p. 210.

[11] *The Horse and His Boy* (New York: Macmillan, 1954), pp. 169–170.

Although God manifests himself in Narnia in the form of a real lion, there is a chameleon-like inconsistency in the size and appearance of this lion. In *The Horse and His Boy* Aslan appears to be no more than a large cat when he comforts a lonely little boy named Shasta, who is hiding among the tombs at night (p. 71). In a different situation in the same book, Aslan runs so swiftly that two runaway children think there are two fierce lions chasing them on opposite sides of the road. Thus he forces them together despite their mutual distrust (p. 24). Again, Aslan appears to Shasta shining like the morning sun and taller than his horse (pp. 139–40).

In the other books there are similar variations in Aslan's revelations of himself. The first time Jill sees him in *The Silver Chair* he is lying with his head raised and his two forepaws out in front, like the lions in Trafalgar Square (p. 16). When he comes to her at the conclusion of the story, he has become so bright and real and strong that everything else begins at once to look pale and shadowy in comparison (p. 202). In *The Magician's Nephew* Digory returns from a difficult assignment and finds Aslan bigger and more beautiful and more brightly golden and more terrible than he had thought him before (p. 119).

In *Prince Caspian* Aslan himself gives part of the explanation for his changeability. Lucy had just been reunited with him after a long separation:

> "Aslan," said Lucy, "You're bigger."
> "That is because you are older, little one," answered he.
> "Not because you are?"
> "I am not. But every year you grow, you will find me bigger"
> (p. 117).

Lewis seems to believe that the more spiritually mature a person becomes, the greater the capacity for comprehending the grandeur and goodness of God. In his book *The Great Divorce*, souls must even develop the ability to enjoy the grandeur and goodness of heaven.[12]

---

[12] New York: Macmillan, 1946, pp. 55–56.

The great Lion has not been divested of godly omnipotence in his animal form, any more than he has lost his grandeur or goodness. Of course he makes it clear that he, too, conforms to basic laws. In one conversation he asks Lucy reproachfully, "Do you think I wouldn't obey my own rules?"[13] One must remember, however, that in Lewis's concept of nature there can be supernatural rules which subordinate ordinary rules.

Aslan could leap with a single bound over high castle walls; the blast of his roaring would bend the trees like grass in a breeze and the stream of his breath could blow a person thousands of miles through the air. He is powerful—yet he is all tenderness. In *Prince Caspian* he roared, "And now, where is this little Dwarf . . . who doesn't believe in lions?" and pounced upon the Dwarf, picking him up in his mouth like a mother-cat does a kitten, shaking him till his armor rattled. Then he tossed him up in the air and caught him gently in his huge velveted paws and set him back on the ground. He asked the breathless Dwarf, no longer cynical, to be his friend (pp. 128–29).

In *The Lion, the Witch and the Wardrobe* Lucy and Susan, already his friends, are privileged to a whole romp with Aslan. When it is over, they are no longer tired or hungry or thirsty. Lucy could never decide whether it was more like playing with a thunderstorm or playing with a kitten (p. 133).

Although Aslan occasionally granted such familiarity to his special followers, his awesome majesty was never diminished. Their feelings toward him could best be summarized by a portion of the dialogue from *The Wind in the Willows*: "Afraid?" murmured the Rat, his eyes shining with unutterable love. "Afraid! Of *Him*? O, never, never! And yet—and yet—O, Mole, I am afraid!" (p. 136).

This reverential dread is not unwarranted in Lewis's constructions. His own concept of the nature of Christ is more severe than the popular concept of today. Lewis contradicts what he terms the common idea that Christ preached a simple and kindly religion which was cor-

---

[13] *The Voyage of the "Dawn Treader,"* p. 132.

rupted into something cruel and complicated by St. Paul. He proposes that in fact all the most terrifying texts are from the lips of the Lord and that those which are more indicative of the salvation of all persons have come from St. Paul.[14]

So it is that Aslan is a stern as well as a loving and kind personality. When in *The Lion, the Witch and the Wardrobe* the Beavers are trying to explain Aslan to the children, the girls are frightened to learn that he is not a human, but a lion. One of them ventures that she would feel rather nervous about meeting a lion. The Beaver answers that such was to be expected, because if any could appear before Aslan without their knees knocking, they must be unusually brave or else just silly. The girl asks if he was, then, unsafe. Mr. Beaver replies, "Who said anything about safe? 'Course he isn't safe. But he's good. He's the king, I tell you" (p. 64).

God's Authority

The attempt to reconcile Christianity with other religions is attacked by Lewis in *The Last Battle* when the Narnians are told that the kingship of Aslan did not discount Tash, pagan god of the Calormenes: "Tash is only another name for Aslan. All that old idea of us being right and the Calormenes wrong is silly. We know better now. The Calormenes use different words but we all mean the same thing." Tash and Aslan were only two different names for "you know who," and there could never be any quarrel between them. Tash was Aslan, Aslan was Tash. Aslan meant no more than Tash (pp. 37–39).

When King Tirian tries to ask how the terrible god Tash who fed on the blood of his people could possibly be the same as the good Lion by whose blood all Narnia was saved, he is attacked by soldiers and taken away. Soon everyone is taught to speak of "Tashlan." The dreadful results of this deception culminate in the eventual appear-

---

[14] "Introduction" to J. B. Phillips, *Letters to the Young Churches: A Translation of the New Testament Epistles* (New York: Macmillan, 1948), p. ix.

ance of Tash, a type of the eschatological Antichrist figure mentioned in the letters of John. Aslan gives over the Tash worshipers to the monster they had promoted. "Thou shalt have no other gods before me" (Ex 20:3).

Aslan displayed his uncompromising, fearfully demanding nature when Jill first met him in *The Silver Chair*. He was displeased with her for her behavior to her companion. Now she was alone and very thirsty. She found a stream, but the great strange lion stood between her and the water. With a heavy, golden voice he bade her come and drink if she was thirsty. Finally she admitted to him that she was nearly frantic with thirst. Again he bade her drink. Awkwardly, she asked him to go away while she drank, but his only answer was a look and a very low growl.

> "Will you promise not to do anything to me, if I do come?" said Jill.
>
> "I make no promise," said the Lion. . . .
>
> "Do you eat girls?" she asked.
>
> "I have swallowed up girls and boys, women and men, kings and emperors, cities and realms," said the Lion. It didn't say this as if it were boasting, nor as if it were sorry, nor as if it were angry. It just said it.
>
> "I daren't come and drink," said Jill.
>
> "Then you will die of thirst," said the Lion.
>
> "Oh dear!" said Jill, coming another step nearer. "I suppose I must go and look for another stream then."
>
> "There is no other stream," said the Lion (p. 17).

Of course Jill's thirst overcame her reluctance and was immediately quenched by the amazingly cold and refreshing water. It cleared her thinking so that she yielded to the Lion and stood before him to admit that she had done wrong. Then he told her the purpose for which he had called her out of her own world. Jill objected to this idea, explaining that she had not been called. She had called out and asked for a way of escape, then found an open door which let her into this other land. "You would not have called to me unless I had been calling to you," said the Lion (p. 19).

The Calvinistic idea of God seeking out his own followers rather than the followers seeking God on their own initiative is basic to Lewis's thought. Lewis agrees with Newman that we are not merely imperfect creatures who must be improved: we are rebels who must lay down our arms.[15] As followers of the greatly contrasting "Quaker tradition of Christian mysticism"[16] have expressed this proposition, religion is God's concern, not ours. He is the Aggressor, the Invader, the Initiator. He is urgently, actively breaking into time and working through those who allow him to lay hold upon them.[17]

In "The Shoddy Lands" God is not allowed to lay hold upon the woman whose mind is being explored. A patient knocking can be heard by the visitor, and with the knocking comes a voice which turns his bones to water: "Child, child, child, let me in before the night comes."[18]

Aslan's pursuit of those he loves recalls Francis Thompson's unrelenting Hound of Heaven:

> Fear wist not to evade as Love wist to pursue.
> Still with unhurrying chase,
> And unperturbed pace,
> Deliberate speed, majestic instancy,
> Came on the following Feet,
> And a Voice above their beat—
> "Naught shelters thee, who wilt not shelter Me."
>
>   ✻   ✻   ✻
>
> Now of that long pursuit
> Comes on at hand the bruit;
> That Voice is round me like a bursting sea:
> "And is thy earth so marred,

---

[15] *The Problem of Pain* (New York: Macmillan, 1948), p. 79.

[16] Walsh, *C.S. Lewis, Apostle to Skeptics*, p. 171.

[17] Thomas R. Kelly, *A Testament of Devotion* (New York: Harper, 1941), pp. 97–99.

[18] *The Best from Fantasy and Science Fiction*, Sixth Series, p. 165.

Shattered in shard on shard?
Lo, all things fly thee, for thou fliest Me!"

✻   ✻   ✻

Halts by me that footfall:
Is my gloom, after all,
Shade of his hand, outstretched caressingly?
"Ah, fondest, blindest, weakest,
I am he Whom thou seekest!
Thou dravest love from thee, who dravest Me." [19]

Shasta is brought face to face with this pursuit in *The Horse and His Boy*. He was riding a sluggish horse aimlessly along a narrow mountain road in the middle of the night. The mists were so thick that he did not know he was winding along the edge of a precipice. He had no idea where the road would take him. Gradually he became aware of a large presence pacing along between him and the gorge. He could not make his horse break into a gallop to escape, so finally he whispered, "Who are you?" The creature answered, "One who has waited long for you to speak." The Thing breathed warmly on his hands and face to assure him that it was not something dead. Then he told it of his many misfortunes and of all the lions that had chased him on his adventures (pp. 136–38).

"There was only one lion," the Voice declared. "I was the lion" (p. 138). After recounting his part in Shasta's adventures, the Voice answered Shasta's bewildered question, "Who *are* you?"

> "Myself," said the Voice, very deep and low so that the earth shook; and again "Myself," loud and clear and gay; and then the third time "Myself," whispered so softly you could hardly hear it and yet it seemed to come from all round you as if the leaves rustled with it (p. 139).

---

[19] *The Hound of Heaven* (Mt. Vernon, New York: Peter Pauper), pp. 6, 20, 22–23.

"I AM THAT I AM," God had answered to that question asked by Moses in the Old Testament (Ex 3:14).

Then the morning came and when Shasta glanced at the Lion's face he slipped out of the saddle and fell at its feet. The strange and solemn perfume of its mane was all round him, as the High King above all kings stooped and touched his forehead with its tongue. Then in a swirl of brightness the Lion disappeared and all that was left was a deep paw print in the grass. It brimmed full of water and soon a little stream was running down the hill (pp. 140–41).

Shasta refreshed himself in the same extremely cold, clear water that Jill's thirst had driven her to taste under such different circumstances at the beginning of *The Silver Chair*. This seems to be the same water that issued from the white rock of protection during the last battle in Narnia. It was so delicious that while the doomed children were drinking they were perfectly happy and could think of nothing else.[20]

Aslan deals with each individual in a unique way to bring every person to the same place. But he does not give an account of his relations with any one person to any other person. When asked, he always answers, "I am telling you your story, not hers. I tell no-one any story but his own."[21] As Christ said when asked, "What about this man?", ". . . what is that to you? Follow me!" (Jn 21:22, RSV).

The most unique individual approach to Aslan is that of Emeth, a Calorman who claimed that he would gladly die a thousand deaths if he might look once on the face of Tash. He passed through the fatal door to the hovel in which Tash was supposedly dwelling and found himself in a fair land which he thought might be the country of Tash. But as he sought Tash he met Aslan and fell at his feet expecting death. At the sight of Aslan he realized that he had been mistaken in serving Tash all of his days. Nevertheless, he felt that it was better to see the Lion and die than to be emperor of the world and not have seen him.

---

[20] *The Last Battle*, p. 131.
[21] *The Horse and His Boy*, pp. 140–41.

God's Love

When Aslan welcomed him, Emeth confessed that he was no son of his, but the servant of Tash. Aslan answered, "Child, all the service thou hast done to Tash, I account as service done to me." When the truth constrained Emeth to say that he had been seeking Tash all his days, Aslan assured him that unless his desire had been for Aslan, he would not have sought so long and so truly—"For all find what they truly seek." [22] Christ had said, "Seek and ye shall find" (Mt 7:7).

After his conversion Emeth declared, ". . . my happiness is so great that it even weakens me like a wound. And this is the marvel of marvels, that he called me Beloved. . . ." [23] Unknown to him at the time of his conversion, he had already passed into the afterlife by passing through the door.

In every story there is found the same indescribable, almost ecstatic, joy and beauty at the climax when one has really met Aslan. It is the answer to that desire expressed so longingly by St. Augustine in *The Confessions*: "Oh! that I might repose on thee! Oh! that thou wouldest enter into my heart and inebriate it, that I may forget my ills and embrace thee, my sole good!" (I. v). The bitterness of Swinburne's lines: "Thou hast conquered, O pale Galilean, / The world has grown grey from thy breath" is completely contradicted by the rich golden joy exhaled by Aslan.

Lewis writes that the person who has passed through the experience of catastrophic conversion feels like one who has waked from nightmare into ecstasy. Like an accepted lover, he feels that he has done nothing, and never could do anything, to deserve such astonishing happiness. Buoyant humility results. [24]

Before writing his children's books, Lewis had attested:

---

[22] *The Last Battle*, p. 166.

[23] *Ibid.*, p. 167.

[24] *English Literature in the Sixteenth Century*, p. 33.

> The deception is . . . in that prosaic moralism which con-
> fines goodness to the region of Law and Duty, which never
> lets us feel in our face the sweet air blowing from "the land
> of righteousness," never reveals that elusive Form which if
> once seen must inevitably be desired with all but sensuous
> desire—the thing (in Sappho's phrase) "more gold than
> gold." [25]

Aslan was solid and real and warm and there was lion-strength
magic in his mane. When Lucy buried her face in it she became brave.
It was beautiful, rich and shining. Ever since the girls first saw him,
they longed to bury their hands in the sea of fur and stroke it. The
wonderful qualities of Aslan's mane and his embrace and his warm
breath remind one of the ecstatic peace which the princess always
found in the arms of her fairy grandmother with long golden hair in
George MacDonald's *The Princess and the Goblin*.

As the Quaker mystic Thomas Kelly has expressed this personal
experience with God,

> One emerges from such soul-shaking, Love-invaded times
> into more normal states of consciousness. But one knows
> ever after that the Eternal Lover of the world, the Hound
> of Heaven, is utterly, utterly real and that life must hence-
> forth be forever determined by that Real. Like Saint Augus-
> tine one asks not for greater certainty of God but only for
> more steadfastness in him. [26]

The power of the physical manifestations of Aslan's love is clearly shown in the passage in *The Magician's Nephew* in which Digory des-
perately dared to entreat Aslan for some cure for his dying mother
back in our world. In despair he looked up at Aslan's face and was
shocked at what he saw:

---

[25] *George MacDonald*, pp. 21–22.
[26] *A Testament of Devotion*, p. 57.

39

For the tawny face was bent down near his own and (wonder of wonders) great shining tears stood in the Lion's eyes. They were such big, bright tears compared with Digory's own that for a moment he felt as if the Lion must really be sorrier about his Mother than he was himself. "My son, my son," said Aslan. "I know. Grief is great. Only you and I in this land know that yet. Let us be good to one another"(p. 127).

After Aslan told Digory what he must do to rectify the troubles of Narnia, he drew a deep breath, leaned down and gave him a lion's kiss. And Digory felt new strength and courage at once, unmindful of the fact that Aslan had made him no promises about his mother.

C.S. Lewis constantly preaches that love is something more stern and splendid than mere kindness. As he explains in *The Problem of Pain*, "Kindness, merely as such, cares not whether its object becomes good or bad, provided only that it escapes suffering." Speaking of the love of God, he asserts that if God is love, God is by definition something more than mere kindness. It appears that though God has often rebuked us and condemned us, God has never regarded us with contempt. God has paid us the intolerable compliment of loving us in the deepest, most tragic, most inexorable sense (p. 29).

The question of ungodly persons does not arise within the original Christian experience. When people try to build a system, says Lewis, very troublesome problems and very dark solutions appear.[27]

God's Justice and Mercy

The love of Aslan for his creation causes him to grant it justice. In *Prince Caspian* the sound of his faraway roar awakens the slumbering soldiers in the camp of the evil king and they stare palely in one another's faces and grasp their weapons. They can sense that vengeance is coming (pp. 129–30). In this book the end of the evil people is sim-

---

[27] *English Literature in the Sixteenth Century*, p. 33.

ple defeat in battle. In some of Lewis's other books, however, the fate of rebels is of more complex spiritual significance.

Uncle Andrew, for example, the foolishly wicked magician of *The Magician's Nephew*, refused to hear anything except growlings and roarings when Aslan spoke. Aslan was unable to teach him the folly of his thinking or to comfort him in the distress he brought upon himself.

This kind of situation is decried in *The Great Divorce*:

> Good beats upon the damned incessantly as sound waves
> beat on the ears of the deaf, but they cannot receive it. Their
> fists are clenched, their teeth are clenched, their eyes fast
> shut. First they will not, in the end they cannot, open their
> hands for gifts, or their mouths for food, or their eyes to see
> (p. 127).

"Oh Adam's sons, how cleverly you defend yourselves against all that might do you good!" Aslan exclaimed.[28] He then gave the silly old man the only gift the man was still able to receive in his terrified state, that of sleep and temporary peace. After his harrowing adventures in Narnia, Andrew finally learned his lesson and never again tried magic when he was returned to his own world. But he was still a vain, foolish old man.

In *The Last Battle* a group of Dwarfs exasperatingly refused to accept any of the good things that were offered to them because of their obsession against being "taken in." The Dwarfs are for the Dwarfs, they would stubbornly repeat. Aslan gave them up to themselves at last, explaining that they had chosen cunning instead of belief. "Their prison is only in their own minds, yet they are in that prison; and so afraid of being taken in that they cannot be taken out. But come, children. I have other work to do" (p. 150).

The villain of *The Horse and His Boy* is even more cruel and proud than Uncle Andrew and comes to a more ignominious end. This selfish Prince Rabadash is given every chance to repent and receive mercy

---

[28] *The Magician's Nephew*, p. 153.

at the hands of the good kings he had wronged. All that Aslan asked him to do was to forget his pride, for he had nothing to be proud of, and his anger, for no one had done him wrong. In answer, Rabadash grimaced and shrieked. He called Aslan a demon and cursed all of Narnia with fiery eloquence. His tirade was ended only as, after repeated warnings from Aslan, he turned into a ridiculous donkey (pp. 185–87).

But even this punishment is tempered with mercy. Rabadash would at an appointed time resume his original shape, though he would always be restricted to a ten-mile radius around the temple in his city. Therefore he could no longer go to war and was always the laughingstock of his country. Lewis's philosophy of dealing with sin is that of Thomas More: "The devill . . . the prowde spirite . . . cannot endure to be mocked." [29]

Aslan used physical affliction in a more serious manner to effect the cure of sin as well as the punishment of sin. In *The Voyage of the "Dawn Treader"* Eustace is turned into a dragon because of his irresponsibility, childishness and selfishness. In the form of this ugly beast he learns to value his friends and to help others. Tolkien says that the dragon "has the trade-mark *Of Faërie* written plain upon him." As a boy, he "desired dragons with a profound desire. . . . The world that contained even the imagination of Fafnir was richer and more beautiful, at whatever cost of peril." [30] The peril for Eustace is that of being left alone on the island, stranded by his size.

One night a huge lion came to him. He shut his eyes tight, but the lion told him to follow and he could not disobey. They went to a mountain garden with a well in the center. There were marble steps going down into it and Eustace was sure that the clear water would ease the pain in his leg. But the lion told him that he must undress first.

Eustace realized that this must mean for him to shed his dragon skin and he found that it came off easily. But as he entered the pool

---

[29] As quoted in C.S. Lewis, *The Screwtape Letters* (New York: Macmillan, 1943), p. [7].

[30] "On Fairy Stories," p. 63.

again, he saw that he was covered with another skin like the first one. Three times he peeled off his dragon skin, only to find another one underneath. Then the lion told him that he must let the lion undress him. Eustace was afraid of the claws, but he submitted. The lion tore deep and the pain was excruciating, but when it was over, Eustace was clean. The water smarted at first, but then it felt delicious and he realized that he had become a boy again. But he was a new boy.[31]

Lewis believes that acknowledging one's sinful condition and being willing to be delivered from any carnal determent to spiritual well-being are essential to conversion. In his imaginative book *The Great Divorce*, Lewis tells about a ghost who had a little red lizard riding on his shoulder, whispering in his ear. A flaming angel offered to relieve him of the little monster, but he was reluctant to have it killed for fear of being hurt himself. As the angel approached, the ghost cried out in distrust because he was being burned. The angel explained, "I never said it wouldn't hurt you. I said it wouldn't kill you" (p. 101). When the distraught ghost finally submitted, he was delivered from the reptile and transformed into a radiant young man.

The inability of Eustace and of the ghost to cleanse themselves is true of all people and illustrates the doctrine in Lewis's chapter in *Mere Christianity* entitled "Nice People or New Men." Nasty people, if they make any attempt at goodness at all, learn more quickly than naturally good people that they need help. "It is Christ or nothing for them" (p. 166).

The sin of traitorous Edmund in *The Lion, the Witch and the Wardrobe* was paid for more dearly than that of Eustace. Edmund had joined the forces of the White Witch and was saved by the followers of Aslan just as she was about to murder him in return for his services. The next morning Aslan and Edmund went walking together and when they returned Edmund was a different person. What Aslan had said to him, no one else ever knew (p. 112).

But soon the witch appeared, claiming the traitor as her lawful prey.

---

[31] *The Voyage of the "Dawn Treader,"* pp. 88–91.

The magic which the Emperor had put into Narnia at the beginning decreed that for every treachery she would have a right to kill. She renounced her claim on Edmund's blood only when Aslan offered himself as substitute (pp. 114–15). As Lewis explains in the Psyche myth of *Till We Have Faces*, "In the Great Offering the victim must be perfect" (p. 56).

Aslan's atonement for Edmund's sin took place at the great Stone Table that very night. He surrendered himself to a howling and gibbering crowd of evil spirits and monsters, who bound him tightly and sheared away his luxurious mane. Then they jeered and mocked him and put a muzzle on his face. Throughout his torment he never moved.[32]

Such a scene is described by Lewis in *Dymer:*

> That moment in a cloud among the trees
> Wild music and the glare of torches came.
> On sweated faces, on the prancing knees
> Of shaggy satyrs fell the smoky flame,
> On ape and goat and crawlers without name,
> On rolling breast, black eyes and tossing hair,
> On old bald-headed witches, lean and bare.
>
> They beat the devilish tom-tom rub-a-dub;
> Lunging, leaping, in unwieldy romp,
> Singing Cotytto and Beelzebub,
> With devil dancers mask and phallic pomp,
> Torn raw with briars and caked from many a swamp
> They came, among the wild flowers dripping blood
> And churning the green mosses into mud (p. 82).

After the diabolical crowd had its fill of expressing its frenzy by kicking and spitting upon the lion, they hoisted him onto the Stone Table. There the witch told him gloatingly that his sacrifice was in

---

[32] *The Lion, the Witch and the Wardrobe*, p. 125.

vain because next she would kill Edmund. Then she plunged a great stone knife into his lion heart.[33]

While the two girls kept vigil over his body during the night, hundreds of little mice came and nibbled away his bonds. Then as the girls watched the sun rise they heard a great noise from the direction of the Table. They turned and saw that it had been rent from one end to the other into two pieces. The body was gone. Just as they expressed their grief, Aslan spoke to them from behind. He had been resurrected, his rich golden mane restored (p. 134).

Tolkien says that

> It is the mark of a good fairy-story, of the higher or more complete kind, that however wild its events, however fantastic or terrible the adventures, it can give to child or man that hears it, when the "turn" comes, a catch of the breath, a beat and lifting of the heart, near to (or indeed accompanied by) tears, as keen as that given by any form of literary art and having a peculiar quality.[34]

The "turn" of this fairy story is the resurrection of Aslan:

> You can say that Christ died for our sins. You may say that the Father has forgiven us because Christ has done for us what we ought to have done. You may say that we are washed in the blood of the Lamb. You may say that Christ has defeated death. They are all true. If any of them do not appeal to you, leave it alone and get on with the formula that does. And, whatever you do, do not start quarrelling with other people because they use a different formula from yours.[35]

The point that Lewis insists upon is that mere time can never wash out the guilt. That can be done only by repentance and the blood of

---

[33] Ibid., p. 126.

[34] "On Fairy Stories," p. 81.

[35] Lewis, Mere Christianity, pp. 141–42.

Christ. Even this, however, cannot cancel the *fact* of a sin, because all times are eternally present to God. Therefore, if we repent of our sins we should remember the price of our forgiveness and remain humble.[36] Edmund's memory of his own past mistakes made it easier for him to be patient and eager to forgive others from that time on.

Although the Gospels culminate in these two phases of Christ's activities, his death and resurrection, the epistles of St. Paul tell us that Christ was also the Creator:

> For by him were all things created, that are in heaven and that are in earth, visible and invisible, whether they be thrones, or dominions, or principalities, or powers: all things were created by him and for him (Col 1:16).

God's Creativity and Care

The genesis of Narnia occurs in *The Magician's Nephew*. When the children and their strange companions accidentally arrived at Narnia, it was Nothing. They found themselves in an expanse of cold dry darkness. At last a voice began to sing far away, the most beautiful noise they had ever heard. Then the sky burst full of stars, all singing in cold, tingling, silvery voices which joined the First Voice. As the children watched, the Voice sang a whole world into existence, part by part, and color by color. When they saw the Singer, it was a Lion (pp. 87–90).

After the Lion had created a host of animals from the ground, he went to and fro among them, occasionally selecting a pair and touching their noses with his own. When all of the chosen ones had gathered around him, Aslan stared hard at them and they all changed. The small ones grew larger, a few of the great ones grew smaller and many stood up on their hind legs. Then he breathed out a long warm breath,[37] there was a flash like fire,[38] and the deepest, wildest voice they

---

[36] *The Problem of Pain*, p. 49.
[37] Cf. Genesis 27.
[38] Cf. Acts 23.

had ever heard said, "Narnia, Narnia, Narnia, awake. Love. Think. Speak. Be divine waters" (p. 103). All of the magical woods people came forth. "Creatures, I give you yourselves," continued Aslan in his strong, happy voice. "I give to you forever this land of Narnia. I give you the woods, the fruits, the rivers. I give you the stars and I give you myself" (p. 105).

By this creative power and his consequent death and resurrection, Aslan almost completely fills the description of Christ in the first chapter of Hebrews:

> God ... hath in these last days spoken unto us by his Son, whom he hath appointed heir of all things, by whom also he made the worlds; who being the brightness of his glory and the express image of his person and upholding all things by the word of his power, when he had by himself purged our sins, sat down on the right hand of the Majesty on high ... (1:1–3).

But after Aslan's resurrection, he did not simply retire to the side of the Emperor Beyond the Sea. "He'll be coming and going," the children were told. "One day you'll see him and another you won't. He doesn't like being tied down—and of course he has other countries to attend to. It's quite all right. He'll often drop in. Only you mustn't press him. He's wild, you know. Not like a *tame* lion." [39] When Aslan dropped in this way, it was usually to instruct, guide or correct his subjects.

Aslan employed "eye-for-an-eye, tooth-for-a-tooth" punishment for purposes of instruction when he appeared one time to Aravis in *The Horse and His Boy*. When she ran away from home, she had cast her stepmother's slave into a drugged sleep, for which the young girl was beaten. Aslan tore Aravis's back with his claws so that her scratches were equal to the stripes on the slave's back. He explained to her later that she needed to know what it felt like and she understood (p. 171).

---

[39] *The Lion, the Witch and the Wardrobe*, p. 149.

Sometimes just the sight of Aslan was enough to make the children aware of their mistakes and guide them in their adventures. In *The Silver Chair* Jill had been distracted from her mission by greedy ambition and had forgotten the set of clues that Aslan had so carefully taught her. He appeared to her one night in a dream, full of sweetness, and although she didn't know what it was that troubled her, she began to weep. Then, to her horror, he asked her to repeat the forgotten signs. He took her to the window and she saw in the moonlight the directions she had failed to follow (p. 98).

When Jill's assignment was finally completed, Aslan returned to her to bring her home. She wanted to tell him how sorry she was for all of her mistakes, but she could not speak. Drawing her close, he touched her pale face with his tongue and said, "Think of that no more. I will not always be scolding . . . " (p. 202). It is clear that although Lewis has incorporated in Aslan the stringent discipline of the Old Testament Jehovah, he has also attributed to him the Old Testament promise "For I will not contend forever, nor will I always be angry . . . " (Is 57:16, RSV).

The God of the Bible was the guardian and guide of God's people in their physical afflictions as well as their spiritual wanderings. One of the times when Aslan appeared in such a way was at the Dark Island in *The Voyage of the "Dawn Treader."* The ship was lost in a great darkness and the men aboard were growing panicky. Lucy whispered a plea to Aslan. Soon a whirring light appeared in the air; it was an albatross. It led them out into the light, and before it left, Lucy heard Aslan's voice whisper courage to her and felt him breathe a delicious smell in her face (pp. 156–57).

In this book the children voyaged to the end of the world, hoping to reach Aslan's land. At last they came to the place where the earth meets the sky. They waded ashore from the Silver Sea and found waiting for them a Lamb so white that even with their eyes as strong as eagle eyes they could hardly look at it. There were fish there roasting on a fire for their breakfast, and, as in the Gospel story, the Lamb said, "Come and have breakfast" (Jn 21:12). After the most delicious food they had ever tasted, Lucy asked the Lamb if this was the way to Aslan's country.

The Lamb answered that for these children the door into Aslan's country was from their own world:

> "There is a way into my country from all the worlds," said the Lamb; but as he spoke his snowy white flushed into tawny gold and his size changed and he was Aslan himself, towering above them and scattering light from his mane (p. 209).

He promised that he would be telling them all the time how to get into his country. He would not tell them how long or short the way would be—only that it would lie across a river. Yet he is the great Bridge Builder.

> "But there I have another name. You must learn to know me by that name. This was the very reason why you were brought to Narnia, that by knowing me here for a little, you may know me better there" (p. 209).

The implication is that when the children returned to their own world they would carry with them concepts which would help them to understand Christ. First would be the recognition of his authority and an acceptance of the doctrine of Incarnation. They would easily realize that incarnation does not divest Christ of his omnipotence and awesomeness. As Queen Lucy says after the Last Battle, "In our world too, a Stable once had something inside it that was bigger than our whole world." [40] His fusion of sternness and gentleness would be comprehensible because of their past experiences with Aslan. Christ would be acknowledged as the initiator of love, and surrender to his love would be known as true joy. The multiple nature of Christ would seem natural. His function as creator, judge, redeemer, instructor and provider would all be related as aspects of the expression of God's love for humankind.

---

[40] *The Last Battle*, p. 143.

NARNIA ROUNDEL
by Patrick Wynne

This roundel includes Aslan, Fledge and the magic wardrobe in a design
reminiscent of C.S. Lewis's Celtic Heritage.

CHAPTER FOUR

POSSIBLE GODS
AND GODDESSES: LEWIS'S
CONCEPT OF HUMANITY

"There was once a little princess who—"
"But, Mr. Author, why do you always write about princesses?"
"Because every little girl is a princess."
"You will make them vain if you tell them that."
"Not if they understand what I mean."
"Then what do you mean?"
"What do you mean by a princess?"
"The daughter of a king."
"Very well, then every little girl is a princess . . ."[1]

This passage from George MacDonald's *The Princess and the Goblin* serves not only as the beginning of a fairy tale, but as the starting point of C.S. Lewis's concept of persons. All of Lewis's teachings about human life are based upon this fundamental spiritual reverence for

---

[1] MacDonald, *The Princess and the Goblin*, p. 1.

individuals. Lewis feels that next to the Blessed Sacraments one's neighbor is the holiest object presented to the senses.

In his book *The Weight of Glory* Lewis says that the glory of one's neighbor is so heavy that only humility can carry it—it will break the backs of the proud. It should be laid on each of us daily. This weight is the realization that we live in a society of possible gods and goddesses. He explains that even the dullest and most uninteresting person may some day be a creature which you would be tempted to worship if you saw it now or else a horror and a corruption such as is seen only in a nightmare. He concludes, "All day long we are, in some degree, helping each other to one or other of these destinations."[2] Lewis's symbolical books are designed to help people toward what he considers the right destination.

Human Behavior

According to critics of modern poetry, myths define the relationship of humans to themselves and to God in such a way that there is no distinction between symbol and meaning. A distinction grows, however, as the civilization declines. Before the separation is complete, mythologies may be used by laypeople and artists to describe a person's place in the universe. "In this sense, a mythology may serve as a guide, explaining conduct and regulating ethics on both material and spiritual planes."[3] Lewis's series of children's books fill this capacity. The structure of all of their mythical plots is the problem of human behavior.

The philosophy behind Lewis's presentation of human problems in an unfamiliar point in space and time is not, as might be supposed, what Lewis calls the idea of the Unchanging Human Heart.[4] In *The*

---

[2] *The Weight of Glory,* pp. 14–15.
[3] Kimon Friar and John Malcolm Brinnin, *Modern Poetry* (New York: Appleton-Century-Crofts, 1951), pp. 421–22.
[4] *A Preface to Paradise Lost,* p. 61.

Pilgrim's Regress Lewis attacks that method satirically by letting his shameless Mr. Sensible advocate the idea that people are always the same although dress and manners vary like shifting disguises.[5] In *A Preface to Paradise Lost* Lewis suggests a more valuable approach to literature: "Instead of stripping the knight of his armour you can try to put his armour on yourself . . ." (p. 62). This is the approach which his books naturally evoke from the reader. He seeks to show the reader how it would feel to have the honor, wit, royalism and gallantries of the characters depicted.

The medieval ideal of chivalry and knighthood is venerated throughout Lewis's writing. Lewis believes that this old tradition is practical and vital. It taught the great warrior humility and forbearance, and it demanded valor of the urbane and modest person. Lewis feels that if we cannot produce brave yet gentle Lancelots we will produce people who are either brutal in peace or cowardly in war. Then the world will be divided between wolves who cannot understand and sheep who cannot defend the things which make life desirable.[6]

The first evidence of knightly behavior in the Narnia Chronicles occurs when the boy Peter saves his sister's life by attacking a monstrous wolf with his sword and slaying it. "Peter did not feel very brave; indeed, he felt he was going to be sick. But that made no difference to what he had to do."[7] Afterwards, Aslan surprises him by causing him to kneel, striking him with the flat of the blade and titling him Sir Peter Fenris Bane. When the children have conquered the rest of their adversaries in this adventure, they are crowned the four rulers of Narnia and reign in chivalric fashion for many happy years.

In this system they gradually grow and change, like the person in a story Lewis tells in *Mere Christianity*. For many years this man had to wear a mask that made him look much more handsome than he really was. When he finally took it off, he discovered that his own face

---

[5] *The Pilgrim's Regress*, p. 86.
[6] "Importance of an Ideal," *Living Age*, CCCLIX (October, 1940), pp. 110–11.
[7] *The Lion, the Witch and the Wardrobe*, p. 106.

had grown to fit it and that he was truly beautiful (p. 146). Similarly, young Peter becomes King Peter the Magnificent, a tall, deep-chested warrior. Susan comes to be Queen Susan the Gentle, a gracious and beautiful woman. Edmund is called King Edmund the Just, because he is great in council and judgment. And little Lucy becomes Queen Lucy the Valiant, the most gay and spirited of all. By following Aslan's will for them, they live together in great joy and richness.

In all of Lewis's stories for children, the will of God proves to be the source of ultimate delight. Throughout *The Pilgrim's Regress*, a book for adults, John seeks the delightful Islands of the West in vain. Only when he ventures the long, difficult journey to the righteous Mountains of the East does he realize that the Mountains of the East are, in fact, the Islands of the West.

In accordance with this theory, obedience is the key to happiness. Aslan uses varying methods to reveal his will to the children in Narnia. In *The Silver Chair* he explains the task he has set before them and charges them to seek to fulfill it until they had done so or died in the attempt or else gone back into their own world. He gives them four signs to guide them on their quest and warns them to repeat the signs over and over every day, letting nothing turn their minds from following them (p. 19).

Aslan gave these directions on his holy mountain. He warned them that the air would thicken as they dropped down to Narnia and they must be careful not to become confused. The signs would not look at all as they would expect them to look; so it was important for them to remember them and pay no attention to appearances. Aslan had spoken clearly to them on the mountain, but he would not often do so down in Narnia.

At other times Aslan did not explain to the children in advance what he wanted them to do. He chose to reveal himself to them and guide them at his own discretion. In *Prince Caspian* the children are journeying through the wilds of Narnia in an attempt to reach the prince in time to save him from destruction. They had made the wrong turn. Suddenly Lucy, who loved Aslan the most, saw him for a moment in the other direction. The other children didn't quite believe her, especially when she said that Aslan wanted them to go the other way:

> "How do you know that was what he wanted?" asked Edmund.
> "He—I—I just know," said Lucy, "by his face" (p. 104).

Despite Lucy's tears, they journeyed on in the wrong direction. Later, when they had realized their mistake, Aslan came to guide them back in the right direction through the night. Lucy was still the only one who could see him and be sure of his presence for a long time. Edmund had more faith than the other two, and eventually he saw the lion shadow, then Aslan himself moving on ahead. It was harder for Peter, who had been very stubborn. Susan was the last of the four to see the great figure, and she was greatly ashamed. It had not been true doubt that had hidden Aslan from her, but fears. This passage demonstrates that sins of attitude can separate people from God (pp. 125–26).

When Lucy encountered Aslan alone, she began to criticize the others for not believing her when she had first seen him. She heard the faintest suggestion of a growl coming from somewhere deep inside him. She apologized.

> "... But it wasn't my fault anyway, was it?" The Lion looked straight into her eyes.
> "Oh, Aslan," said Lucy. "You don't mean it was? How could I—I couldn't have left the others and come up to you alone, how could I? Don't look at me like that ... oh well, I suppose I could. Yes, and it wouldn't have been alone, I know, not if I was with you ..." (pp. 117–18).

Whenever the children had committed any sin by their actions or their thoughts, a look or a word from Aslan was sufficient as a reprimand. It was only in his presence, however, that they fully realized the danger or the seriousness of their shortcomings. They were good children, as judged by common standards, but they fell far short of the total goodness which Aslan's nature seemed to seek for them.

Sin and Evil

According to J.B. Phillips, Christians aspire to a level of life which they are not spiritually robust enough to maintain. They "can see that it is right" and they "can desire, even passionately, to follow the new way, but in actual practice [they do] not achieve this new quality of living." [8]

C.S. Lewis believes that the great sin is the sin of pride or self-conceit. It was through pride that the devil became the devil, the complete anti-God state of mind. Pride leads to every other vice. It gets no pleasure out of having something, only out of having more of it than the next person. Most of the evils which people attribute to greed or selfishness are the result of pride. In *Mere Christianity* Lewis observes that pride is not something that God forbids us because of concern for God's own dignity. God simply wants to eliminate this barrier between God and creation (pp. 94–99).

Because Lewis believes the sin of pride to be the primary force of evil in our own world, it is to be expected that pride is the initial form of evil in his children's books. The introduction of sin into Narnia is in the person of Jadis, the proud, cruel queen of the dead world of Charn. This witch gloried in the power she had once wielded over the greatest city of all worlds and set out to conquer new worlds so that she would have more subjects to honor and obey her. She hated Aslan and did not see him as he really was.

In God, according to *Mere Christianity*, one encounters something which in every respect is immeasurably superior to oneself. As long as one is proud, one cannot know God. "As long as you are looking down, you cannot see something that is above you" (p. 96). This is why Jadis did not recognize Aslan to be the rightful king of Narnia.

---

[8] *Your God Is Too Small* (New York: Macmillan, 1955), p. 132.

Lewis points out that the more pride one has, the more one dislikes pride in others. Jadis exemplified this behavior when she blamed the destruction of Charn upon her sister. "At any moment I was ready to make peace—" she said, "yes, and to spare her life too, if only she would yield me the throne. But she would not. Her pride has destroyed the whole world."[9] Jadis was incapable of realizing that it was her own pride that had caused the tragedy.

This dazzlingly beautiful queen believed that her subjects belonged to her like cattle. Her overweening sense of superiority led her to exempt herself from the common rules of ethics and morality. As she loftily explained this principle to the children, ". . . what would be wrong for you or for any of the common people is not wrong in a great Queen such as I. The weight of the world is on our shoulders. We must be freed from all rules. Ours is a high and lonely destiny."[10]

These same words were spoken by the foolish magician in *The Magician's Nephew* who ranked himself with all profound students and great thinkers and sages, people "like me who possess hidden wisdom" (p. 16). When Digory saw through his uncle's other grand words, he realized that all they meant was that he thought he could do anything he wanted.

Pride is also a common failing of the children. When it occurs, it always keeps them from full fellowship with Aslan. Accordingly, Aslan commended every display of humbleness. Every time he gave someone a commission of honor and responsibility, it was with the attitude that he expressed in *Prince Caspian* by saying, "If you had felt yourself sufficient, it would have been a proof that you were not" (p. 173).

In *The Lion, the Witch and the Wardrobe* it was pride that caused Edmund to deny his experience in Narnia to his brother and sister who had never been there. Afterwards, when all four of them were there togeth-

---

9 *The Magician's Nephew*, p. 53.
10 *Ibid.*, p. 55.

er, he decided that the others were not paying enough attention to him. This was his imagination; but the witch's promise that she would make him a prince was tempting him, so he sneaked away and betrayed the others to her. He had been duped by her flattery.

The other reason Edmund betrayed his true friends was the vice of greed. The witch had fed him enchanted Turkish Delight, which would make the eater desire more and more, even enough to kill him. This food had the opposite effect of Lewis's refreshing Perelandrian science-fiction fruit, which was too delicious to eat for mere self-indulgence. One would not gorge himself on that fruit for fear of vulgarity.[11] But Edmund had become oblivious to vulgarity. He couldn't even enjoy any food that he ate later, because there is nothing that ruins the taste of good ordinary food so much as the memory of bad magic food.[12]

This is only one of the times when the evil enchantment of greed is employed in an attempt to cause the children to sin against Aslan. It also distracted the children from the signs they were following in *The Silver Chair,* when the lovely Lady in green beguiled them with promises of warmth and rich food and ease at the castle of the giants (p. 74). In *The Voyage of the "Dawn Treader"* the children had landed on the island Death-water. There they discovered a pool that turned any object immersed in it to solid gold. Within minutes they were under its curse and began to fight among themselves. Only the distant appearance of Aslan broke the spell and gave them a chance to escape with their old natures intact (pp. 105–06).

Whether the element involved is gold or luxury or food or feminine beauty, enchantments are always brought on by evil disguised as innocent attractiveness. In *The Lion, the Witch and the Wardrobe* Edmund's encounter with the witch (p. 24), which led to his enchantment, is parallel to the story of little Kay meeting the evil snow queen in "The Snow Queen" by Hans Andersen. Both of these witches appear in

---

[11] *Perelandra* (New York: Macmillan, 1952), pp. 38–39.

[12] *The Lion, the Witch and the Wardrobe,* p. 71.

great sledges, dressed in white fur. Both are tall and beautiful and seem almost perfect to the eyes of their little victims; but both are as cold and pale as white ice. As soon as the boys are enchanted, they are no longer afraid. They feel very important, try to show off, and indiscreetly tell anything that is asked of them.

The vague uneasiness experienced in this state is concisely expressed by Andersen when Kay tells the queen that he could do mental arithmetic as far as fractions and knew the number of square miles and the number of inhabitants in the country. The queen always smiled, and then it seemed that what he knew was not enough.[13] This same uncertainty is attributed to Mark Studdock in Lewis's novel *That Hideous Strength* after he joins the league of evil called the N.I.C.E. He is greedy for the things this diabolical organization offers to him, but after he confusedly accepts the terms presented, he feels more inadequate and uneasy than before.

Greed is the first tool of enchantment. The other one, perhaps more important, is the technique of mental confusion and the subjugation of intelligence by emotional persuasion and fallacious rationalization. This is illustrated by the first temptation, that of the apple in the garden in *The Magician's Nephew*. Digory knew that he was forbidden to take the apple of life for any use of his own. He had been told to carry it to Aslan. But as he was leaving, the witch confronted him and told him that if he didn't stop to listen to her he would miss some knowledge that would make him happy all his life. Although Digory knew better, he listened (p. 144).

He withstood the temptation to eat of the fruit himself, but when the witch tried to persuade him that if he really loved his mother he would steal the fruit to heal her, he weakened. She contrasted his rightful devotion to his mother with his thoughtless obedience to a wild animal in a strange world that was none of his business. She made him feel muddled and guilty, but he insisted that he was bound by his promise to the lion, whether it was right or not. Speaking ever-so-

---

[13] Hans Christian Andersen, *Fairy Tales* (New York: Garden City Publishing Co., 1932), p. 142.

sweetly, the witch rationalized away his promise, but made one fatal mistake. She suggested that he could use his magic ring to return to his own world with the apple and leave his friend Polly behind. This meanness made the rest of the witch's reasoning sound false, and suddenly Digory's head cleared (pp. 146–47).

A stronger enchantment is worked and more painfully overcome in *The Silver Chair*. The beautiful witch hides her anger and throws green powder in the fireplace, filling the room with a very sweet and drowsy smell. Then she begins a steady, monotonous thrumming on the strings of her instrument. It becomes very difficult to think. She speaks sweetly and quietly, with a kind, soft, musical laugh. She tells the children, the prince and Puddleglum that the world above the ground that they spoke of is all a dream. Although they rouse themselves several times and try to argue with her, it is easier to succumb and a relief to admit that she is right:

> Then came the Witch's voice, cooing softly like the voice of a wood-pigeon from the high elms in an old garden at three o'clock in the middle of a sleepy, summer afternoon. . . .
>
> "You have seen lamps and so you imagined a bigger and better lamp and called it the *sun*. You've seen cats and now you want a bigger and better cat and it's called a *lion*. Well, "tis a pretty make-believe, though, to say truth, it would suit you all better if you were younger. And look how you can put nothing into your make-believe without copying it from the real world, this world of mine which is the only world" (pp. 151–53).

The trick of lulling the victim's reasoning powers to sleep is advocated by Screwtape in his letters to Wormwood. "By the very act of arguing," says Screwtape, "you awake the patient's reason; and once it is awake, who can foresee the result?" The business of the tempter is to fix the victim's attention upon the stream of immediate sense experiences. "Teach him to call it 'real life' and don't let him ask what he means by 'real.'" [14] The devils fear to let humans think about the realities they can't touch and see. The goal of Satan is befuddlement.

"There is nothing like a good shock of pain for dissolving certain kinds of magic," Lewis observes when the spell of the witch is broken.[15] Puddleglum, in one last desperate attempt against the wiles of the witch, stamped the fire with his bare feet. The pain cleared his head, the smell cleared the heads of the others, and the disruption infuriated the witch.

Her magic undone, the witch reverted to her hideous serpent form. This transformation is similar to one that occurs in *The Place of the Lion* by Charles Williams (pp. 170–71). Her arms merged into her sides, and her legs were intertwined with each other as she became a writhing pillar of poison green. All of her face disappeared except the elongated nose and flaming eyes, browless and lashless. The prince slew this thick serpent as it coiled its loathsome body around him for the kill. Lewis teaches that the enchantment of evil can be overcome, but that it demands strength, self-sacrifice and clear thinking. Evil is a paradox of beauty and horror, and destroys people by deceiving them.

Aslan has no patience with people who blame enchantments for their failures. In *The Magician's Nephew* Digory had struck a magic bell, despite the warning below it, because he was curious. He had told his friend Polly, "I expect anyone who's come as far as this is bound to go on wondering till it sends him dotty. That's the Magic of it, you see. I can feel it beginning to work on me already" (p. 45). Then he fought with her when she tried to constrain him. When he gives an account of his actions to Aslan, he adds that he thinks he must have been a bit enchanted by the writing under the bell.

> "Do you?" asked Aslan; still speaking very low and deep.
> "No," said Digory, "I see now I wasn't. I was only pretending" (p. 121).

---

[14] *The Screwtape Letters*, p. 12.
[15] *The Silver Chair*, p. 154.

Unprincipled curiosity, the Faustian lust for knowledge, causes many of the troubles in this series. It is Uncle Andrew's insatiable greed for wisdom, not tempered with any sense of moral responsibility, that leads to the original invasion of Narnia by the evil Queen Jadis. Lewis refers to the motivation of magicians in his *English Literature in the Sixteenth Century*, the third volume in *The Oxford History of English Literature*:

> . . . We see at once that Bacon and the magicians have the closest possible affinity. Both seek knowledge for the sake of power (in Bacon's words as "a spouse for fruit" not a "curtesan for pleasure"), both move in a grandiose dream of days when Man shall have been raised to the performance of "all things possible" (p. 13).

Queen Jadis herself, in *The Magician's Nephew*, is the paramount example of this perversion, causing the destruction of the world of Charn by acquiring knowledge that she is not meant to wield. It is the secret of the Deplorable Word. She tells the children proudly:

> "It had long been known to the great kings of our race that there was a word which, if spoken with the proper ceremonies, would destroy all living things except the one who spoke it. But the ancient kings were weak and soft-hearted and bound themselves and all who should come after them with great oaths never even to seek after the knowledge of that word. But I learned it in a secret place and paid a terrible price to learn it" (p. 54).

Whatever price Jadis paid, the price paid by the rest of her race is higher. Aslan told the children when they returned to their own world that the race of Adam and Eve must take warning from this example.

> "But we're not quite as bad as that world, are we, Aslan?"
> "Not yet, Daughter of Eve," he said. "Not yet. But you are growing more like it. It is not certain that some wicked

one of your race will not find out a secret as evil as the Deplorable Word and use it to destroy all living things . . ." (p. 160).

The insinuation here about weapons of international warfare is the most specific symbolic commentary upon a social problem in current affairs to be found in Lewis's books for children.

Many other problems of individual behavior are handled in these books. These include vanity, spying, theft, frivolity, quarreling, prudishness and bullying. Their imaginative treatment embodies the traditional Christian attitude toward such sins, but presents it in a lively narrative manner.

One of these problems is stressed more than any of the others. It is the problem of cowardice. Cowardice, Lewis contends, is the only vice which is purely painful. People have become proud of most vices, but not of this one. Hatred has its pleasures, so it is often the compensation by which people reimburses themselves for their fear and shame.[16]

"Perfect love, we know, casteth out fear. But so do several other things—ignorance, alcohol, passion, presumption and stupidity."[17] Courage is the only acceptable answer to fear and it is chief of the virtues. Lewis agrees with Johnson that where courage is not, no other virtue can survive except by accident.[18] "A chastity or honesty, or mercy, which yields to danger will be chaste or honest or merciful only on conditions. Pilate was merciful till it became risky."[19]

Heroism and Hierarchy

The most courageous character in Narnia is a large talking mouse named Reepicheep. He exemplifies knightly valor to the point of foolhardiness, but Aslan favors him for this fearlessness. He is intro-

---

[16] *Screwtape Letters*, p. 147.

[17] "*The World's Last Night*," p. 23.

[18] *Surprised by Joy*, p. 153.

[19] *The Screwtape Letters*, pp. 148–49.

duced in *Prince Caspian* as a gay and martial mouse with a tiny rapier at his side and long whiskers which he twirls like a moustache. His speech of allegiance to the prince is given with the flair, made ludicrous by his small size, which characterizes his every speech and action: "'There are twelve of us, Sire,' he said with a dashing and graceful bow, 'and I place all the resources of my people unreservedly at your Majesty's disposal'" (p. 65).

Reepicheep is at the fore of every battle, but the culmination of his career is his journey to the utter East, to the land of Aslan. His life's ambition is to venture to the end of the world and never return. In *The Voyage of the "Dawn Treader"* he fulfills this daring ambition. His attitude toward adventure is summarized in his challenging answer to the question of what use it would be to sail into the mysterious blackness of the Dark Island:

> If by use you mean filling our bellies or our purses, I confess it will be no use at all. So far as I know we did not set sail to look for things useful but to seek honour and adventures. And here is as great an adventure as ever I heard of and here, if we turn back, no little impeachment of all our honours (p. 150).

The antithesis of this attitude is expressed in *The Pilgrim's Regress* by Mr. Sensible. He advocates moderation in all things, claiming that the secret of happiness lies in knowing where to stop. Travel should serve to quiet, without satiating, a liberal curiosity and to provide interesting memories. But when it comes to crossing a canyon, a modest tour along one side is sufficient and much less dangerous (p. 100). Thus, with irony, Lewis has expressed for adults the lesson which Reepicheep expresses more directly.

It is Reepicheep who partakes of the food and drink offered to the travelers at an enchanted table to prove its safety. When they had asked the girl there how they could know that she was a friend, she had answered, "You can't know. . . . You can only believe—or not."[20]

---

[20] *The Voyage of the "Dawn Treader,"* p. 169.

Reepicheep always dares to believe. He finds answers by direct experience.

When at last he leaves the others to go on alone, he knows that he will need his sword no longer; so he casts it into the lilied sea, where it stands upright with its hilt above the surface. This Arthurian symbolism ratifies him as the ideal of Christian valor. As he bids his friends good-bye he tries to be sad for their sakes, but he is trembling with happiness.

Thirty-three years before the publication of *The Voyage of the "Dawn Treader,"* Lewis published a poem titled "Our Daily Bread," which includes these stanzas anticipating the story of Reepicheep:

> Often me too the Living voices call
> In many a vulgar and habitual place,
> I catch a sight of lands beyond the wall,
>   I see a strange god's face.
>
> And some day this will work upon me so
> I shall arise and leave both friends and home
> And over many lands a pilgrim go
>   Through alien woods and foam,
>
> Seeking the last steep edges of the earth
> Whence I may leap into the gulf of light
> Wherein, before my narrowing Self had birth,
>   Part of me lived aright.[21]

The ultimate reward of courage or of love (which, as the virtue which casts out fear, is related to courage), is justified by Lewis at the beginning of *The Weight of Glory,* where he stresses the positive aspect of virtue:

> If you asked twenty good men to-day what they thought the
> highest of the virtues, nineteen of them would reply,

---

[21] *Spirits in Bondage,* pp. 86–87.

Unselfishness. But if you asked almost any of the great Christians of old he would have replied, Love. You see what has happened? A negative term has been substituted for a positive and this is of more than philological importance. The negative ideal of Unselfishness carries with it the suggestion not primarily of securing good things for others, but of going without them ourselves. I do not think this is the Christian virtue of Love. The New Testament has lots to say about self-denial, but not about self-denial as an end in itself. We are told to deny ourselves and to take up our crosses in order that we may follow Christ; and nearly every description of what we shall ultimately find if we do so contains an appeal to desire. If there lurks in most modern minds the notion that to desire our own good and earnestly to hope for the enjoyment of it is a bad thing, I submit that this notion has crept in from Kant and the Stoics and is no part of the Christian faith (p. 1).

"Goodness, armed with power, is corrupted; and pure love without power is destroyed."[22] This statement by Reinhold Niebuhr in *Beyond Tragedy* expresses Lewis's attitude toward Christianity and government. Lewis openly embraces the maxim "All power corrupts." He goes on to say, "The loftier the pretensions of the power, the more meddlesome, inhuman and oppressive it will be. Theocracy is the worst of all possible governments."[23] In Narnia the government is divinely ordained, but it is not a theocracy. It took the form of an oligarchy which later became a monarchy.

Lewis believes in political equality, though only because of its protective function. He distinguishes between two views of democracy. What he calls the false, romantic doctrine is the theory that all peo-

---

[22] Sayers, *The Mind of the Maker*, p. 201.

[23] "Lilies That Fester," *Twentieth Century*, CLVII (April, 1955), 335. Also available in *The World's Last Night and Other Essays* (1960), pp. 31–49, and *They Asked for a Paper* (1962), pp. 105–19.

ple are so good and so wise that they deserve a share in the government and the government needs their advice. Lewis holds rather that fallen people are too wicked to be trusted with any irresponsible power over each other.[24] His answer is "Let us wear equality; but let us undress every night."[25]

Corruption and bureaucracy are not tolerated in the series for children. In *The Last Battle* Shift, the ape, comes into power by telling the naïve donkey, "You know you're no good at thinking, Puzzle, so why don't you let me do your thinking for you?" (p. 12). The outcome of Puzzle's submission is the destruction of Narnia.

When Prince Caspian found a similar situation in his Lone Islands, he overthrew the governor by force, in a scene rather like that of Christ cleansing the temple.[26] The major social evil which he revoked was that of slavery. The governor insisted that the Prince didn't understand the economic problem involved. Caspian replied that he didn't see that slavery brought to the islands any food, drink, books, music, horses or other objects worth having and that it was to be stopped.[27] Lewis does not disagree with Aristotle's statement that some people are fit only to be slaves. But he rejects slavery because he sees no one fit to be an owner:[28]

> "But that would be putting the clock back,"[29] gasped the governor. "Have you no idea of progress, of development?"
> "I have seen them both in an egg," said Caspian. "We call it *Going bad* in Narnia. . . ."[30]

There is little reference to politics in this series of children's books,

---

[24] *The Weight of Glory*, p. 77.

[25] "Equality," *Spectator*, CLXXI (August 27, 1943), 192.

[26] *The Voyage of the "Dawn Treader,"* p. 45.

[27] *Ibid.*, p. 48.

[28] "Equality," p. 192.

[29] In the chapter "We Have Cause to be Uneasy" in *Mere Christianity*, Lewis points out that if the clock is wrong, putting it back is often a sensible thing to do (p. 22).

[30] *The Voyage of the "Dawn Treader,"* p. 48.

because Lewis feels that only a sick society must think much about the subject, as sick people must think about their digestion. Digestion and politics are the means to an end, not an end in themselves. The end of the secular community is to facilitate and safeguard the family, friendship and solitude. Lewis quotes Dr. Johnson in saying that the end of all human endeavor is to be happy at home.[31] This is the secular end of all behavior in Narnia.

Lewis glorifies the state of kings and queens and feels that they are an asset to society. He contends, "Where men are forbidden to honour a king they honour millionaires, athletes, or film stars instead: even famous prostitutes or gangsters. For spiritual nature, like bodily nature, will be served; deny it food and it will gobble poison!"[32]

There was responsibility for the rulers of Narnia as well as glory, however. As the voyagers neared the end of the world, Prince Caspian decided to go on with Reepicheep instead of returning to his kingdom in Narnia. Only when Aslan personally commanded him to let the others go on and to return alone to Narnia did Caspian tearfully realize that he had no choice. Lewis expresses this principle in a commentary upon the works of William Morris:

> In the later romances the claims of the tribe are not forgotten and the young hero who goes to the end of the world to drink of the well of life carries thither with him and carries back, the determination to settle down and be a good king in his own small country. No wanderings are allowed to obliterate our love for "the little platoon we belong to."[33]

The return to Narnia in *The Voyage of the "Dawn Treader"* was not really sad for Caspian, because the beautiful girl of the enchanted table, the daughter of a star, was waiting for him to take her back with him as his bride. This is the only incident involving romantic love in the

---

[31] *The Weight of Glory*, p. 32.

[32] "Equality," p. 192.

[33] C.S. Lewis, "William Morris," *Rehabilitations and Other Essays* (London: Oxford, 1939), p. 50.

Narnian series. The prince, hoping to break the enchantment of three sleeping lords, had told the girl of the story in our world in which the prince couldn't break the enchantment until he had kissed the princess. "But here," she answered, "it is different. Here he cannot kiss the princess till he has dissolved the enchantment" (p. 170). This gentle repartee was the extent of their courtship as recorded by Lewis. The lack of emphasis upon romantic love in the Narnia stories is intentional—they were written for children—but it is fairly typical of all of Lewis's writing. Notable exceptions are the novel *That Hideous Strength*, his personal account of the death of his wife Joy in *A Grief Observed*, and his studies of Courtly Love, the love poetry of Donne and the role of romantic love in Christian morality.

His only commentary upon family life in the Narnia books is at the beginning of *The Voyage of the "Dawn Treader."* He describes the home environment of Eustace Clarence Scrubb, a priggish, nasty little boy who almost deserved his unhappy name. His father and mother had taught him to call them by their Christian names, which Lewis considers a perverse notion. It is, he says, an effort to ignore the difference in kind which makes for real organic unity.[34] These parents were vegetarians, nonsmokers and teetotallers and wore a special kind of underclothes. Very little furniture graced their house and there were few bedclothes and open windows. They did not want an ordinary son.

As a result of his progressive rearing, Eustace preferred animals dead and pinned on cards. He liked only books of information, preferably those illustrated with pictures of grain elevators or fat foreign children doing exercises in model schools (p. 1). Lewis laments this approach to learning: "The hours of unsponsored, uninspected, or perhaps even forbidden reading, the ramblings and 'long, long thoughts' in which those of luckier generations first discovered literature and nature and themselves, are a thing of the past."[35]

---

[34] *The Weight of Glory*, pp. 34–35.
[35] "Lilies That Fester," pp. 336–37.

In *The Silver Chair* Lewis caustically describes Eustace's school (p. 1). It was very progressive, unruly and corrupt. The other extreme, a dull, stiff, authoritarian girls' school in Narnia is exposed just as mercilessly in *Prince Caspian* (pp. 166–67). Lewis states his conservative attitudes on child training and education in "The World's Last Night": "For my own part I hate and distrust reactions not only in religion but in everything. Luther surely spoke very good sense when he compared humanity to a drunkard who, after falling off his horse on the right, falls off it next time on the left" (p. 2).

A subject less commonly discussed than love, family relations and education demands more of Lewis's attention. It is the problem of the position of animals in society and their relation to humankind.

The use of anthropomorphic beasts is discussed by William Empson in his consideration of *Alice in Wonderland*. He says that the talking-animal convention and changes of relative size evidently make some direct appeal to the child even though more sophisticated ideas are piled into them. Ever since Aesop, talking animals have been used for didactic purposes.[36] But in Lewis's books there is a real concern for the animals themselves. Tolkien claims that talking beasts in fairy tales are founded on "the desire to converse with other living things," which is "as ancient as the Fall." He says that a vivid sense of the separation between humans and beast is very ancient, but also a sense that it was a severance and that a guilt lies on us. "Other creatures are like other realms with which Man has broken off relations and sees now only from the outside at a distance, being at war with them, or on the terms of an uneasy armistice."[37]

Lewis seems to have been influenced by the domestic nature attributed to animals by other writers. We might note, for example, the following passage from Hans Christian Andersen:

"Will you fly out free?" asked the Princess, "or will you

---

[36] William Empson, *Some Versions of Pastoral* (Norfolk, Connecticut: James Laughlin, New Directions, 1935), p. 265.

[37] "On Fairy Stories," p. 80.

have fixed positions as court crows, with the right to everything that is left in the kitchen?"

And the two Crows bowed and begged for fixed positions, for they thought of their old age and said, "It is so
good to have some provisions for one's old days."[38]

The character of these crows is like the character of the beaver couple in *The Lion, the Witch and the Wardrobe*. The beavers are tidy, provincial
people of modest means who value security.

In real life Lewis did not grant animals the wealth of sacred indi-
viduality which they enjoy in his fancies. He classified humans as the
only amateur animals; all the others are professionals:

They have no leisure and do not desire it. When the cow has
finished eating she chews the cud; when she has finished chew-
ing she sleeps; when she has finished sleeping she eats again.
She is a machine for turning grass into calves and milk—in
other words, for producing more cows ... if they could speak
they would all of them, all day, talk nothing but shop.[39]

In a letter to Lewis, Evelyn Underhill criticized such tame concepts of the animal kingdom:

Is the cow which we have turned into a milk machine or the
hen we have turned into an egg machine really nearer the
mind of God than its wild ancestor? ... Your own example
of the good-man, good-wife and good-dog in the good
homestead is a bit smug and utilitarian, don't you think, over
against the wild beauty of God's creative action in the jun-
gle and deep sea. ... Of course I agree that animals too are
involved in the Fall and await redemption and transfigura-
tion. (Do you remember Luther looking up from Romans

---

[38] *Fairy Tales*, p. 161.
[39] *Rehabilitations*, p. 83.

8:21 and saying to his dog, "Thou too shalt have a little gold-
en tail"?) And man is no doubt offered the chance of being
the mediator of that redemption. But not by taming, surely? Rather by loving and reverencing the creatures enough
to leave them free. . . .[40]

Lewis did not disagree with her. In fact, he incidentally expressed
his sympathy with the wildness and freedom of animals in his poem
about people "Under Sentence":

> There is a wildness still in England that will not feed
> In cages; it shrinks away from touch of the trainer's
> hand;
> Easy to kill, not easy to keep. It will not breed
> In a zoo for the public pleasure. It will not be planned.
>
> Do not blame us too much if we, being woodland folk
> Cannot swell the rejoicing at this new world you
> make;
> We, hedge-hogged as Johnson, we unused to the yoke
> As Landor, surly as Cobbett (that badger), birdlike as
> Blake.
>
> A new scent troubles the air—friendly to you per-
> haps—
> But we with animal wisdom understand that smell.
> To all our kind its message is guns, ferrets, traps,
> And a ministry gassing the little holes in which we
> dwell.[41]

In the Narnian series Lewis neatly fuses these three contrasting
concepts of animals (anthropomorphic domesticity, unimaginative

---

[40] *The Letters of Evelyn Underhill*, ed. Charles Williams (London Longmans, Green, 1943), p. 302.
[41] *Spectator*, CLXXV (September 7, 1945), 219.

productivity and wildness) to inculcate effectively the doctrine of the humane treatment of animals. This is a major fact of human behavior throughout the books. Even so minor an offense as throwing stones at a stray cat is not to be winked at.[42]

In *The Horse and His Boy* a frivolous girl named Lasaraleen obnoxiously spoils her pet monkey. Yet Lewis comments upon the reaction going on at present against excessive love of pet animals. We have been taught to despise the rich, barren woman who loves her dog too much and her neighbor too little. But Lewis reminds us that one can do something for the Peke and it can make some response. It is at least sentient.[43]

In the chapter devoted to animals in *The Problem of Pain* Lewis sums up the convictions on this subject that can be discerned in the Narnian tales. "Man was appointed by God to have dominion over the beasts and everything a man does to an animal is either a lawful exercise, or a sacrilegious abuse, of an authority by divine right" (p. 126). As Aslan said to the first king and queen, in *The Magician's Nephew*, "You shall rule and name all these creatures and do justice among them and protect them from their enemies . . ." (p. 123).

"The Chief End of Man"

To summarize, Lewis believes first in the sanctity of people and in the will of God as the first principle of human behavior in relation to God, to one's fellow humans, and to animals. Obedience to God's will depends upon fellowship with God and results in chivalric behavior. Sin is inevitable, and the first sin is pride. Greed, intellectual sloth, lust for knowledge and cowardice are the other major sins. The counterpart of the last of these, courage, is the first of the virtues. It is no secret that virtue will be rewarded. Consideration for the welfare of the individual and conservatism are advocated in human relations.

---

[42] *The Horse and His Boy,* p. 74.
[43] *The Personal Heresy,* p. 67.

Although the divine right of monarchy would be the ideal system of human rule, in our sinful state no one should wield irresponsible power over their neighbors. Humans have been granted power over animals, however, and must use it wisely. These points are the key to Lewis's concept of human life on this earth. But his total concept of humankind is not limited to this life.

Lewis acknowledges that we cannot help wishing that human life and youth would last forever, yet he questions the wisdom of that wish. He refers to the dialectic of natural desire which William Morris hinted at when he said that life owes all its sweets to that same death whence rise all its bitters. Without the gift of death, life would become a wearisome torment.[44] An unlimited extension of life as we know it now would not be a blessing. "Neither the individual nor the community as popular thought understands them," says Lewis in *The Weight of Glory*, "can inherit eternal life: neither the natural self, nor the collective mass, but a new creature" (p. 42).

This idea is illustrated at the end of *The Silver Chair* when Old Caspian has died in Narnia. His friends, on the Mountain of Aslan, heard the distant, despairing funeral music and found the dead king lying on the golden gravel of a stream, with the water flowing over him and swaying his long white beard. They wept for him, and the Lion wept too. Then Aslan told the Son of Adam to pierce his paw with a great pointed thorn. A large drop of blood splashed into the stream over the body. It changed, becoming younger and younger, then leaped up before them as a young man or a boy. In Aslan's country people have no particular ages. Lewis contends that even in this world, it is the stupidest children who are most childish and the stupidest grown-ups who are most grown-up.

In *The Last Battle* the transformed bodies of the children are described. They were all cool, fresh and clean, with splendid, yet comfortable, clothes and faces somehow nobler than ever before. All of their physical infirmities had disappeared, along with their ages.

[44] *Rehabilitations*, p. 51.

Although the new Caspian was strong and joyous after his resurrection, the children were apprehensive because they knew he had died. Aslan told them good-naturedly that most people have died. He had himself. Then Caspian told them that he would be a ghost if he appeared in Narnia again, but one can't be a ghost in one's own country. The best part of it was that Caspian could no longer want wrong things, and whatever he did would be right.[45]

The forces of evil could no longer affect him. Even the rebellion and eternal condemnation of the sinful witch could no longer infect his happiness. Lewis denies

> the demand of the loveless and the self-imprisoned that they should be allowed to blackmail the universe: that till they consent to be happy (on their own terms) no one else shall taste joy: that theirs should be the final power; that Hell should be able to veto Heaven.[46]

At the end of Narnia millions of creatures, all of the living people and beasts of that world, came streaming toward the doorway where Aslan waited. As they approached him, some of their faces filled with fear and hate. And these swerved to his left, disappearing into his huge black shadow. Those who loved him came in at the Door at his right.

Later, inside, Aslan turned to the children and said that they did not look so happy as he meant them to be. They answered that they were greatly afraid of being sent away, because they had been sent back into their own world so often.

> "No fear of that," said Aslan. "Have you not guessed?"
> Their hearts leaped and a wild hope rose within them.
> "There *was* a real railway accident," said Aslan softly.
> "Your father and mother and all of you are—as you used

---

[45] *The Silver Chair*, p. 205.
[46] *The Great Divorce*, p. 124.

to call it in the Shadowlands—dead. The term is over: the holidays have begun. The dream is ended: this is the morning." [47]

So it is that Lewis's concept of human life is climaxed in death. One of his favorite quotations from the pen of George MacDonald expresses it best:

"You have tasted of death now," said the Old Man. "Is it good?"

"It is good," said Mossy. "It is better than life."

"No," said the Old Man. "It is only more life." [48]

[47] *The Last Battle*, p. 183.

[48] *George MacDonald*, p. 104.

CHAPTER FIVE

WEAVING A SPELL

Do you think I am trying to weave a spell? Perhaps I am; but remember your fairy tales. Spells are used for breaking enchantments as well as for inducing them. And you and I have need of the strongest spell that can be found to wake us from the evil enchantment of worldliness which has been laid upon us for nearly a hundred years.

These words from *The Weight of Glory* (p. 5) aptly apply to Lewis's books for children. They are counteractive to the spirit of worldliness. Although these books are richly sensuous, this characteristic is merely an expression of the spiritual values symbolized. Lewis finds the same element in Scriptural imagery. He believes that "the scriptural picture of heaven is . . . just as symbolical as the picture which our desire, unaided, invents for itself; heaven is not really full of jewelry any more than it is really the beauty of nature or a fine piece of music." [1] In *The Great Divorce* Lewis adds, "The picture is a symbol: but it's truer than any philosophical theorem (or, perhaps, than any mystic's vision) that claims to go behind it" (p. 129).

---

[1] *The Weight of Glory*, p. 6.

Lewis's View of His Fairy Tales

Lewis's own definition of his books for children would perhaps be "fantasy that hovers between the allegorical and the mythopoeic."[2] He feels that myth-making may be an art or gift which criticism has largely ignored:

> It may even be one of the greatest arts; for it produces works which give us (at the first meeting) as much delight and (on prolonged acquaintance) as much wisdom and strength as the works of the greatest poets. . . . It goes beyond the expression of things we have already felt. It arouses in us sensations we have never had before, never anticipated having, as though we had broken out of our normal mode of consciousness and "possessed joys not promised to our birth". It gets under our skin, hits us at a level deeper than our thoughts or even our passions, troubles oldest certainties till all questions are reopened and in general shocks us more fully awake than we are for most of our lives.[3]

When he wrote this paragraph Lewis was speaking not of his own mythopoeic works, but of those of George MacDonald. He proceeded to consider the problem of whether or not this art is a species of literary art. Because a particular pattern of events composes the myth, not a particular arrangement of words, Lewis assumes that any other effective means of communication would be equally legitimate.[4] Concerning stories, Lewis suggests that the internal tension between the theme and the plot constitutes its chief resemblance to life. In real life, as in a story, something must happen. Lewis says that that is the trouble: "We grasp at a state and find only a succession of events in which the state is never quite embodied. . . ."[5] In stories the plot is

---

[2] *George MacDonald*, p. 14.

[3] *Ibid.*, pp. 16–17.

[4] *Ibid.*, pp. 14–15.

[5] "On Stories," p. 105.

only a net whereby to catch the real theme. This usually is something other than a process, with no sequence in it and much more like a state or quality such as giantship, otherness or the desolation of space.[6]

Lewis feels that "the Christian will take literature a little less seriously than the cultured Pagan." Unbelievers often attach an almost religious significance to their aesthetic experiences and have to obey their artistic consciences like mystical amoral laws. They often feel a superiority to the great mass of people who turn to books for mere recreation. In contrast, Christians know that "the vulgar, since they include most of the poor, probably include most of [their] superiors." They know "that the salvation of a single soul is more important than the production or preservation of all the epics and tragedies in the world." Therefore they do not object to tales and comedies for mere amusement and refreshment.[7]

Lewis credits the humanists with the mistakenly serious approach to literature. They could not really bring themselves to believe that the poet cared about the shepherds, lovers, warriors, voyages and battles. They must be only a disguise for something more "adult." The Medieval readers had also believed in a poet's hidden wisdom, but they did not allow the hidden wisdom to obscure the fact that the text before them was "a noble and joyous history." Perhaps this was because they had been taught that the multiple meanings of Scripture never abrogated the literal sense. They pressed the siege, wept with the heroine and shuddered at the monsters.[8]

"All children's books are on a strict judgement poor books," Tolkien has said. "Books written entirely for children are poor even as children's books."[9] Lewis would agree. He holds that

> no book is really worth reading at the age of ten which is
> not equally (and often far more) worth reading at the age of

---

[6] *Ibid.*, p. 102.
[7] *Rehabilitations*, p. 195.
[8] *English Literature in the Sixteenth Century*, p. 28.
[9] "On Fairy Stories," p. 59.

fifty—except, of course, books of information. The only imaginative works we ought to grow out of are those which it would have been better not to have read at all. A mature palate will probably not much care for *creme de menthe:* but it ought still to enjoy bread and butter and honey.[10]

His own books for children appeal to adults as well as children and are enjoyable even when read for mere amusement and refreshment in their literal meaning.

According to Lewis, the fundamental difference between the Christian writer and the unbeliever in their approach to literature is that the Christian will ask of every idea and every method not "Is it mine?", but "Is it good?"[11] In the preface to *The Allegory of Love* Lewis states, ". . . I am well aware, like the philosopher, that 'if I had succeeded in owing more, I might then perhaps have gained more of a claim to be original'."[12]

Lewis's View of Truth

It is true that there is little original material in Lewis's books for children. He tapped many literary sources for the fanciful frameworks of his stories. Most of the Christian convictions expressed within these frameworks are traditional Christian beliefs freshly stated. Lewis believed in the divine creation of nature and humankind, the subsequent corruption of both of them and the personal love of God which redeems them.

Lewis's credo, we have seen, can be divided into three major categories: his opinions about nature, God and humankind. These opinions establish Lewis's position in the areas of philosophy, theology, psychology and sociology.

---

[10] "On Stories," p. 100.

[11] *Rehabilitations*, p. 195.

[12] London: Oxford, 1936, p. [vii].

Lewis's concept of nature is threefold. It consists of a romantic appreciation of untamed beauty, a rational acceptance of the supernatural and a realistic awareness of the corruption and ultimate destruction of our present system. His concept of God is that of a creator, redeemer and sustainer who is omnipotent, omniscient and omnipresent. This personal God of love, simultaneously an awesome authority figure, has the power to be revealed to creation by assuming an incarnate form. Lewis's concept of humankind is based upon people's relationship to God. Therefore it is reverential, yet critical. Humanity is prone to sin and this keeps people from the full joy of fellowship with God. People should resist the deceptions of evil and determine their behavior toward God, other people and animals by love. The resurrected person will enjoy an eternal life of unbroken fellowship with God. These three concepts have been graphically presented in mythological form in the Narnian tales.

Lewis expressed his feeling about mythology in relation to Christianity in *The Pilgrim's Regress,* the first book he wrote after becoming a Christian. This book has never enjoyed the popularity of many of his later works, but it was the source of the ideas in most of them.[13] At the end of his adventures the pilgrim is in the caverns and Wisdom troubled him by saying that his experiences had been only figurative, nothing other than mythology. Then another voice, noticeably like that of Aslan, spoke to him, saying:

> "Child, if you will, it *is* mythology. It is but truth, not fact: an image, not the very real. But then it is My mythology. The words of wisdom are also myth and metaphor but since they do not know themselves for what they are, in them the hidden myth is master, where it should be servant: and it is but of man's inventing. But this is My inventing, this is the veil under which I have chosen to appear even from the first until now. For this end I made your senses and for this end your imagination, that you might see my face and live" (pp. 219–20).

---

[13] Walsh, *C.S. Lewis, Apostle to Skeptics,* p. 49.

ANDREW KETTERLY

PART TWO

EXPLORING THE NARNIAN CHRONICLES

This guide provides a wide variety of information and ideas for personal pleasure, for instruction and for spiritual nurture.

NOTE:

The Narnian Chronicles were first read in the order of publication and cherished that way, but for forty years opinion has been divided about whether that order remains the best. The latest edition, from HarperCollins, switches the books to the order of their inner chronology. We can be sure that C.S. Lewis wouldn't care. On April 23, 1957, he sent his opinion to an American boy named Laurence Krieg, who made Lewis's letter public in the January 1973 issue of *Mythprint* (page 11).

> The problem of whether to read the Narnia books in the order in which they were written or in the order of Narnian chronology bothered me at a tender age and my mother, who was in correspondence with C.S. Lewis at the time asked him what he thought; she suggested reading them in order of publication, while I firmly believed they should be read in the Narnian chronology. Lewis answered [me] as follows:
>
> > I think I agree with your order for reading the books more than your mother's. The series was not planned beforehand as she thinks . . . so perhaps it does not matter very much in which order anyone reads them. I'm not even sure that all the others were written in the same order in which they were published. I never keep notes of that sort of thing and never remember dates.

BOOK ONE

THE MAGICIAN'S NEPHEW

The Main Theme: Weakness to Power

The characters in *The Magician's Nephew* moved from weakness to power—or at least tried to do so.

Anyone with spunk wants power. Some seek power to do good and others seek it to do evil. Some seek power in rebellion and others seek it in faithfulness and obedience.

Digory longed for the power to do good, to save his mother's life. Temptation to seize that power wrongly almost destroyed him and his mother. He finally gave up and thus enabled Aslan to work the miracle that was needed. This is a great paradox: power sometimes exists in submission.

Uncle Andrew was obsessed and poisoned by lust for occult power, the selfish power and pride of secret knowledge. He was cured of that addiction in old age and lived out his days a weak and foolish but more innocent man.

Jadis was obsessed and poisoned by addiction to political power; she is the kind who would rather rule in hell than enjoy heaven. She could not stand not being more powerful than God. Her "deplorable word," a weapon of ultimate destruction, is what this kind of power is bound to lead to in the end. "I will either control or destroy" is the motto of inner weakness.

Frank and Nellie enjoyed their transformation from hard-working but poor Londoners into the first king and queen of Narnia, appointed to rule justly and defend bravely with the power of their sound minds and good hearts.

Strawberry enjoyed his transformation from a tired old cab-horse to a powerful winged horse who could soar over mountains.

Digory's mother was transformed from a physically helpless, dying invalid into a strong, happy woman who had the power to enjoy life and nurture her family again.

"Think of me, Boy," the witch warned Digory, "when you lie old and weak and dying. . . ." Perhaps the fear of death is the deepest root of all distorted uses of power. Helplessness and physical death is a fearful thought for most people. It is a thought that most people like to avoid. This is part of the human condition; angels are not mortal, and animals don't have to think about their own mortality. Only humans try to defend themselves from the fear of weakness and death.

Seizing illegitimate power is an attempt to avoid weakness (even the ultimate weakness, death), but it is a false escape. Like plucking and eating fruit at the wrong time and in the wrong way, seizing illegitimate power is poison. The only way to receive power without harm is to receive it humbly and use it wisely. Good power is a trust from God.

Background of *The Magician's Nephew*

Forty-three years before he wrote *The Magician's Nephew*, nine-year-old "Jack" Lewis watched his lovely mother weaken, suffer and die of cancer. She died at home on August 23, 1908, her husband's forty-fifth birthday; and that home was never really happy again. She had been the sunshine of the family. When Lewis wrote of Digory's dilemma, he wrote from his own heart.

Lewis had already written five other books about Narnia before he went back to tell about the very beginning of Narnia in this book, which he called *Polly and Digory*. But the publisher left Polly out of the title entirely by choosing *The Magician's Nephew* instead. Which title was better?

When C.S. Lewis was a little boy, Edith Nesbit was publishing her delightful children's books that Lewis loved. Although she had written a great deal for adult magazines, it was not until 1899, the very year when Frank Baum published his first Oz book and when Sigmund Freud published his book about dreams, that E. Nesbit published her first book for children. Those three 1899 books made their authors famous. (Freud pretended that his book came out in 1900 because he thought it would be more impressive that way.)

Nesbit's first book, *The Story of the Treasure Seekers*, told how the Bastable children tried to earn or find money to help support their family. (At that time Nesbit was 41 years old and had long been working to support her own family.) The Bastables appeared again in *The Would-begoods* in 1901 and in *The New Treasure Seekers* in 1904 (when Lewis turned six). During the same period, Nesbit published three wonderful books with magic in them: *Five Children and It* (1902), *The Phoenix and the Carpet* (1904) and *The Story of the Amulet* (1906).

Like E. Nesbit, C.S. Lewis wrote his first book for children when he was middle-aged. And when he wrote *The Magician's Nephew* he was writing about children just the age of Nesbit's story children, old enough to have adventures in 1900. The same food, clothes and setting, and even some similar events were at work. It is no coincidence that in *The Story of the Amulet* the children accidentally brought the queen of ancient Babylon to their home in London and she caused a riot. Lewis openly copied that idea in *The Magician's Nephew*, as if tipping his hat to Nesbit.

The Story of the Amulet began with the words "There were once four children who spent their summer holidays in a white house . . . whose names were Cyril, Robert, Anthea and Jane. . . ." Lewis echoed that in the first sentences of *The Lion, The Witch and the Wardrobe* and *Prince*

Caspian. Near the end of *The Story of the Amulet* Nesbit wrote, "Then out of that vast darkness and silence came a light and a voice. The light was too faint to see anything by and the voice was too small for you to hear what it said. But the light and the voice grew. And the light was the light that no man may look on and live and the voice was the sweetest and most terrible voice in the world. The children cast down their eyes." Lewis echoed that passage in *The Lion, the Witch and the Wardrobe.*

In *The Story of the Amulet* the children's father was in Manchuria and their mother was ill. In *The Magician's Nephew* Digory's father was in India and his mother was ill.

Lewis echoed Nesbit in various other ways also in his Chronicles; for example, Lewis's Tisroc in Calormen sounds like Nesbit's Nisroch in Babylon, which is obviously the picture Lewis had in mind when he invented Tash.

Nesbit was extremely playful in her books. When evil Nisroch came into the story, Cyril asked, "What was that name the Queen said? Nisbeth—Nesbit—something?"

It was similar playfulness, no doubt, that caused Lewis to hint about Nesbit's part in *The Magician's Nephew* and to mark that hint with her fictional family's name and his own name in the third sentence: "In those days Mr. Sherlock Holmes was still living in Baker Street and the Bastables were looking for treasure in the Lewisham Road." It is a true Nesbit-style touch.

Key Symbol: Fruit of the Tree of Life

A forbidden fruit in a magic garden is an ancient image in myth and fairy tales. According to the account in Genesis, this image began at the start of human history. God watered the Garden of Eden with a stream and in the middle of the Garden he put two trees, the tree of life and the tree of knowledge. God told Adam and Eve that if they ate the beautiful fruit from the tree of knowledge they would die. We all know what happened after that.

Then the Lord God said, "Now the man has become like one of us and has knowledge of what is good and what is bad. He must not be allowed to eat fruit from the tree of life and live forever." So the Lord God sent him out of the Garden of Eden and made him cultivate the soil from which he had been formed. Then at the east side of the garden he put living creatures and a flaming sword which turned in all directions. This was to keep anyone from coming near the tree of life (Gen 3:22–24, TEV).

But at the end of the human story as described in the Bible, there are trees of life on both sides of the river in the city of God, with plenty of fruit and no guards.

The angel also showed me the river of the water of life, sparkling like crystal and coming from the throne of God and of the Lamb and flowing down the middle of the city's street. On each side of the river was the tree of life, which bears fruit twelve times a year, once each month; and its leaves are for the healing of nations. Nothing that is under God's curse will be found in the city (Rev 22:1–3, TEV).

The magic fruits are symbols of spiritual power which are poison when taken wrongly and eternal nourishment when taken right. These fruit trees are the very last symbol mentioned in the entire Bible:

"Listen!" says Jesus. "I am coming soon! I will bring my rewards with me, to give to each one according to what he has done. I am the first and the last, the beginning and the end.

"Happy are those who wash their robes clean and so have the right to eat the fruit from the tree of life and to go through the gates into the city. But outside the city are the perverts and those who practice magic, the immoral and the murderers, those who worship idols and those who are liars both in words and deeds.

"I, Jesus have sent my angel to announce these things to you in the churches. I am descended from the family of David; I am the bright morning star." The Spirit and the Bride say, "Come!"

Everyone who hears this must also say, "Come!" Come, whoever is thirsty; accept the water of life as a gift, whoever wants it.

I, John, solemnly warn everyone who hears the prophetic words of this book if anyone adds anything to them, God will add to his punishment the plagues described in this book. And if anyone takes anything away from the prophetic words of this book, God will take away from him his share of the fruit of the tree of life and of the Holy City, which are described in this book (Rev 22:12–19, TEV).

The Magician's Nephew and the Bible

Colossians 1:9–17 (RSV) declares that Christ created our world as well as redeemed it. In this passage Paul prays for the opposite of spiritual stupidity for certain other Christians. He prays for power in their lives. These are key values in *The Magician's Nephew*.

And so, from the day we heard of it, we have not ceased to pray for you, asking that you may be filled with the knowledge of his will in all spiritual wisdom and understanding, to lead a life worthy of the Lord, fully pleasing to him, bearing fruit in every good work and increasing in the knowledge of God. May you be strengthened with all power, according to his glorious might, for all endurance and patience with joy, giving thanks to the Father, who has qualified us to share in the inheritance of the saints in light. He has delivered us from the dominion of darkness and transferred us to the kingdom of his beloved Son, in whom we have redemption, the forgiveness of sins.

He is the image of the invisible God, the first-born of all creation; for in him all things were created, in heaven and on earth, visible and invisible, whether thrones or dominions or principalities or authorities—all things were created through him and for him. He is before all things and in him all things hold together. He is the head of the body, the church; he is the beginning, the first-born from the dead, that in everything he might be preëminent. For in him all the fulness of God was pleased to dwell and through him to reconcile to himself all things, whether on earth or in heaven, making peace by the blood of his cross.

Does Aslan's creation of all things remind you a bit of Christ's creation of all things? Does Polly and Digory's transfer from Charn to Narnia remind you a bit of our deliverance from the dominion of darkness and transference to the kingdom of God's beloved Son? Are Charn and Narnia good images to use sometimes when thinking of spiritual realities?

Special Vocabulary in *The Magician's Nephew*

Lewis knew and enjoyed many uncommon and outdated words. He sprinkled some of these into his Narnian stories, and many readers like to know their definitions:

Bastables: the children in a popular set of books by Edith Nesbit

box window: a rounded bay window

bunk: British school slang meaning to run away

cistern: water storage tank

Colney 'Atch: Colney Hatch was slang, and in 1900 "Colney Hatch for you!" meant "You're crazy!"

counterpane: quilt or bedspread

cove: British slang for man or rogue

dem: polite slang for damn (ironic when you think of Jadis)

frowsy: musty (In *The Silver Chair* Lewis used *fusty*; in *The Horse and His Boy* he used *frowsty*. All three are about the same.)

hansom: a small carriage with two wheels, named after its designer

Hoovers: vacuum cleaners (Lewis uses a common brand name)

jackdaw: a glossy black European member of the crow family

Nellie: a casual form of the name Helen

Pax: British school slang for truce, friendship

showing the white feather: British slang for showing oneself a coward (referring to a white tailfeather in cross-bred gamecocks)

stow it, Guv'nor: slang for "Shut up, fellow"

Tantivy: a cry sometimes used to imitate the sound of a horn or galloping feet

Yeomanry: a cavalry force which became part of the British Territorial Army

A Favorite Quotation in *The Magician's Nephew*

Notice how much all the children learn in the Chronicles.

"Now the trouble about trying to make yourself stupider than you really are is that you very often succeed."

Is there a spiritual danger in playing dumb, as Lewis believed? What are some common reasons for having a closed mind? (Does a closed mind, like a strong city wall, make some people feel safer?)

Favorite Food in *The Magician's Nephew*

There is much mention of food in *The Magician's Nephew* and Lewis's other stories of Narnia. Lewis said he was once accused of putting in food because he knew that children are greatly interested in food. Quite the contrary, he said; he put in food because he enjoyed food himself. Every book of Narnia suggests snacks for readers, although not all the snacks are easy to get and easy to enjoy.

In *The Magician's Nephew* a messy piece of toffee in a boy's pocket was magically transformed into a tree laden with pieces of toffee. (In Edith Nesbit's story "The Mixed Mine," a messy piece of toffee in a boy's pocket was magically transformed into a full pound of toffee.) Toffee is easy to get and most people like it. Ordinary caramels from the grocery store are just about what Lewis meant by toffee. For a more healthful snack, apples are perfect. Even the best earthly apples will seem dull compared to those from the Garden, but they can serve as a reminder of "the real thing." Nuts, with or without honey, are good for celebrating Uncle Andrew's captivity.

When and Where in *The Magician's Nephew*

The Year One is when this story takes place in Narnia.

Notice that on the first day in the world of Narnia all five of these take place: (1) desolation, (2) creation, (3) desecration, (4) celebration, (5) coronation.

This story begins in 1900 in London. Polly is eleven and Digory is twelve. Later in the Chronicles, Lewis tells us with a straight face (and a twinkle in his eye) that when Digory was quite middle aged he was a famous learned man, a professor and a *great traveler*. But we know that any traveling Digory did after he was twelve was limited to this world and would not seem great to him.

Chapters 1, 2—London
Chapters 3, 4, 5—Trip to Charn
Chapters 6, 7, 8—London
Chapters 9, 10, 11—Narnia
Chapters 12, 13—Western Wild
Chapter 14—Narnia
Chapter 15—London

Lewis wrote the Narnian Chronicles for both children and adults. He knew that adults would often read them aloud to children, so he made the chapters the right length for that and kept them all about the same length. Because Lewis sounded the words in his mind as he wrote, his stories flow delightfully when read aloud.

Facts and Ideas about *The Magician's Nephew*

1. *Creation and Re-Creation:* When Digory's mother got well she brought light, music and laughter into the stuffy Ketterly house. She was so playful that her sister-in-law called her a baby; and she had in a sense been reborn. Her light, music and laughter are like faint echoes of Narnian creation.

When the bear fell down after insisting that animals don't fall down, the Jackdaw called that The Third Joke. The First Joke, of course, had been the Jackdaw himself accidentally speaking out of turn. But what was The Second Joke? It was not a blunder like the other two. It was the first bit of wit in Narnia and it was from Aslan himself. Lewis loved humor and there is much of it in his writing. He believed that humor, like justice, is one of God's good gifts to us.

2. *Second Chapter of Acts:* When Aslan breathed on his group of special animals, the scene was a bit like Pentecost. His eyes almost burned them and there was a flash of fire. Then their tongues were set loose. Their first two words were: "Hail, Aslan." The first one to speak out alone and admit that he had a lot to learn was Strawberry.

3. *The Secret Observer:* Sarah came into the story five times, and four of those times Lewis stopped to tell us what a good time she was having. She was the Ketterlys' housemaid. She fetched the cab (perhaps Frank and Strawberry) for Andrew and Jadis; she fetched Digory to help Aunt Letty; she warned the police that Jadis was abroad; and she stood in the doorway watching the commotion and let Digory, Polly and Uncle Andrew slip in unseen after their return from desolation, creation, desecration, celebration and coronation. She thought *she* had a really exciting day!

4. *Point of View:* "You will keep on looking at everything from the wrong point of view," Uncle Andrew complained to Digory before the adventures began. Then when Digory and his friends were going after Aslan, Lewis tells us what the choosing of the animals had looked like from Uncle Andrew's point of view. What you see and hear, Lewis assures us, depends upon what sort of person you are. Uncle Andrew had seen his guinea pigs, before the adventure, as objects to use any way he pleased. Now he saw animals only as a possible threat to his safety. He didn't notice what the animals were really doing, although he watched them closely, because he had no interest in them except a selfish interest.

Lewis once gave advice about how to avoid God. Part of his advice was: "Concentrate on money, sex, status, health and (above all) your own grievances." (That fits Uncle Andrew perfectly.) Later in the essay Lewis remarked, "To some, God is discoverable everywhere; to others, nowhere. . . . Much depends on the seeing eye." This essay is "The Seeing Eye" in Lewis's collection *Christian Reflections.*

Does C.S. Lewis's point of view cause his readers to notice important things?

Factual Quiz Just for Fun

1. Polly Plummer's secret place was (a) Narnia, (b) under the roof of some London row houses, (c) her back garden.

2. The way to the green Wood Between the Worlds was (a) a green ring, (b) a guinea pig, (c) any pool, (d) a yellow ring.

3. The door to the hall of images, the little arch on the pedestal, the bell in the arch, and the hammer, were all apparently (a) gold, (b) silver, (c) iron, (d) lead.

4. Queen Jadis destroyed Charn with (a) slaves and soldiers, (b) the Deplorable Word, (c) a nuclear explosion.

5. Which of these did Jadis *not* do in London? (a) steal pearls, (b) throw Aunt Letty across the room, (c) turn people into dust, (d) wreck a cab, (e) madden a cab horse, (f) break an iron bar, (g) attack the police.

6. At the dark empty place the good Cabby (a) prayed, (b) sang a harvest hymn, (c) cursed his fate.

7. As the Lion sang the new world into existence, which two observers hated him and his song? (a) Strawberry and the Cabby, (b) Uncle Andrew and Jadis, (c) Polly and Digory.

8. Nellie, the Cabby's wife, came to Narnia (a) by magic rings, to find her husband, (b) by Aslan's call, to be a queen, (c) pulled there by Jadis to be her servant.

9. After Digory picked the silver apple in the magic garden he was tempted twice; which was *not* one of his temptations? (a) to eat one of the apples because of hunger and thirst for it, (b) to plant the apple and grow a silver apple tree for himself, (c) to take the apple home to cure his dying mother.

10. Which of the following did *not* grow in the story? (a) a toffee tree, (b) a lamp-post, (c) money trees, (d) ring trees, (e) magic apple trees.

ANSWERS: 1 – b, 2 – d, 3 – a, 4 – b, 5 – c, 6 – b, 7 – b, 8 – b, 9 – b, 10 – d.

Thinking about Feelings

1. How do you feel about experimentation on animals for the satisfaction of human curiosity? Lewis was against it. Was he too soft-hearted about animals? Are you soft-hearted or hard-hearted about animals?

2. Both Andrew and Jadis despised their sisters. If you have a sister or brother, are you able to overcome rivalry and irritations and selfishness when they crop up? If so, how do you manage it?

3. Both the Cabby and Digory's mother loved to sing. The stars in this story were sublime singers. Lewis was not a musician, but he loved some kinds of classical music. (Any music lover who reads *The Magician's Nephew* would do well to listen to "The Creation" by George Frederic Handel [1685–1759]. Some consider it almost as beautiful as his "Messiah.")

4. Have you known anyone who received physical healing in answer to prayer when medical doctors could not help? If so, how did that event affect your feeling toward God? If that person had a relapse and died (as happened to Lewis's wife, Helen Joy Lewis) how would you feel toward God?

5. There are various spiritual sources of alleged physical healing which are not Christian, such as certain occult healing ministries. What do you think about turning to such sources for help in extremely tragic situations?

6. There are scientific and political leaders who feel they are above the rules of decency which apply to common people. "Ours is a high and lonely destiny" was said by both Jadis and Andrew. Have you heard similar claims from any of today's thinkers and experimenters? Would you notice if you did?

7. Do you think there really might be other worlds outside our own space-time system? Is that possibility pleasant or frightening? Are heaven and hell inside or outside our own space-time system?

8. In 1900 Aslan prophesied to Polly and Digory that in our world before long great nations would be ruled by tyrants who care no more for joy and justice and mercy than Jadis did. Can you name tyrants Lewis surely had in mind? Can you see joy and justice and mercy in any specific world leaders or organizations today? Are these qualities of Aslan himself? Aslan told Frank and Helen, "Be just and merciful and brave. The blessing is upon you." Does this apply to everyone who wants to serve God?

The Magician's Nephew as Inspiration

1. *The Journal of the American Scientific Affiliation* is a scholarly publication which aims to present an evangelical perspective on science and the Christian faith. One of its regular features has been a book review section headed by an attractive design. The New Testament is in the center, open to the Gospel of John. Just to its right, next to a calculator and a stone, is a small book entitled *The Magician's Nephew*. What does *Magician's Nephew* have to do with science?

2. In 1976, California musician Steve Brown produced an album called "Lion's Breath" on the Daybreak label. His "Lion's Song" describes Aslan as creator. In 1980 Sparrow Records first produced "The Roar of Love" by a highly respected Christian recording group called The Second Chapter of Acts, featuring Anne Herring. This entire album is composed of songs of Narnia and is available on both tape and compact disk.

3. One summer the Christian education leader of a large church in Southern California started an "Aslan Club" as one of the special summer activities for children. Every Wednesday for seven weeks all the fourth, fifth and sixth graders could come for an hour in the morning to enjoy activities related to their Narnian book of the week.

4. The high school department in that church happened to be going through the Chronicles of Narnia in a different way. Each week leaders would choose a special section from the book of the week and read it aloud to the group on Sunday morning, and then there was discussion about the implications that excerpt has for our lives and beliefs.

5. Every year many individuals and church groups go through the Chronicles of Narnia during Lent. A Trappist monk in South Carolina said once that he had read them three times in the last three years and that for him they were about the most spiritual books he had ever read in his 16 years as a monk. "They are just chuck full of insights into who God is, who we are and how we relate to God and to one another." They go deep into your heart and whole being, he concluded.

Benediction Based on *The Magician's Nephew*

Like Digory, we fear the loss of our securities and loves.
Like Polly, we want to be good sports and good friends.
Like Frank, we wish to return to a simpler way of life.
Like Strawberry, we would like to escape drudgery and grow wings.
In all of this, protect us from wrong use of gold bells and silver apples.
Create in us clean and obedient hearts.

BOOK TWO

THE LION, THE WITCH
AND THE WARDROBE

The Main Theme: Frozen to Thawed

People who live in icy climates know the drama and joy of the coming of spring every year; it is a rebirth of life.

In this story Edmund had a frozen heart, hard with cruelty and selfishness and resentment of his older brother. When he saw a happy young squirrel turned to stone by the White Witch, his heart suddenly changed; he felt sorry for someone besides himself for a change. (When the squirrel was frozen into a statue, Edmund's heart started to melt.)

The inner and outer weather started to change at the same time. There came a sweet chattering, murmuring, bubbling, splashing and roaring of water. Edmund's heart gave a great leap when he realized that Narnia's winter was over.

Water is the symbol of birth and rebirth, and it starts flooding through the story. Just before Aslan's sacrifice, the girls buried their cold hands in the beautiful *sea* of fur and stroked it. In the final chapter, after the costly victory, Aslan and his friends marched along the great river down to the sea itself where the children will reign at Cair Paravel. They came to the sand, with its rocks and little pools of salt water and sea weed and the smell of the sea. There were long miles of bluish-green waves breaking forever and ever on the beach. And the cry of the sea gulls.

Through the Eastern door of Cair Paravel one could hear the voices of the mermen and mermaids swimming close to the castle steps and singing in honor of their new Kings and Queens.

During the riotous scene in the Witch's castle where Spring came to all the creatures who had been frozen in stone, Aslan said "Look alive, everyone," with double meaning. He meant "hurry along," but in a deeper sense he meant "no more of this death for you." He awakened Giant Rumblebuffin and had him break down the gate and set the captives free.

Lewis believed that all paralyzed people will be unfrozen someday.

Background of *The Lion, the Witch and the Wardrobe*

It was about 1914 when the picture of a little goat-man carrying packages in a snowy wood first popped into C.S. Lewis's head. He was 16. As years went by, Lewis changed in all kinds of ways. He went to France to fight in World War One and was wounded there. He won awards as a student at the University of Oxford. He became a professor at Oxford. He became a Christian. He became a successful author. But he never forgot the picture of the Faun in the snowy wood.

During World War Two, some schoolgirls were evacuated from the London area because of the bombing there and were placed in Lewis's home in the suburbs of Oxford. That is where Lewis got his story idea about children boarding at a professor's house in the country. One of these guests has told about sneaking in and out of windows with Lewis's help, but nothing about wandering through any magic wardrobe. His favorite was named Jill. (After he paid her way through drama school, she became an actress and married Clement Freud, grandson of Sigmund Freud and a Member of Parliament.)

So it was that during World War Two he began to write a story that included his picture of the Faun in the snowy wood and the children from London. But the story stopped and he put it aside. He kept busy during the war teaching, writing books and giving popular talks on BBC Radio. His friend Charles Williams died when the war ended. His picture was on the cover of *Time* magazine. And then one day when he was 50 he began to write his story about the Faun in the wood again. To his surprise, this time a great lion named Aslan seemed to leap into the story of his own accord. (Lewis had been having dreams about lions.) He finished the book quickly and called it *The Lion, the Witch and the Wardrobe.* It was his first book for children.

Lewis and a group of his friends who called themselves the Inklings chatted and shared their writing once a week at The Eagle and Child, an Oxford pub nicknamed "The Bird and Baby." Lewis thought that J.R.R. Tolkien's fantasies (*The Hobbit* and *The Lord of the Rings*) were wonderful, but Tolkien disliked Lewis's fantasy *The Lion, the Witch and the Wardrobe.* Lewis went ahead and published it anyway. It came out quietly in 1950 and split the century in half.

On March 5, 1951, Lewis wrote to a correspondent about his new book, glad that she liked it. He told her that a number of mothers and teachers had decided that it was likely to frighten children, so it was not selling very well. "But the real children like it," he added, "and I am astonished how some *very* young ones seem to understand it. I think it frightens some adults, but very few children."

In 1954 Lewis answered an American named Mr. Kinter who asked him where he got the idea of the White Witch. Lewis said that it was no use to ask him. This is the same evil person we find in many fairy tales. "We are born knowing the White Witch, aren't we?" Lewis exclaimed.

Where did Lewis get the idea of the lone London lamppost in a clearing in the woods? Professor M.A. Manzalaoui, who was a pupil of Lewis's, presents his delightful theory in the first footnote in Appendix Two of this book.

In 1956 I wrote to tell Lewis how much the Narnian Chronicles meant to me. "How nice to hear anyone who still believes in adjectives and calls them the 'Narnian' not the 'Narnia' series," he answered.

Twenty years later the *Times* in London took a poll asking the children of England to name their favorite book. First choice was *Charlie and the Chocolate Factory* and second was *The Lion, the Witch and the Wardrobe*. After another twenty years, *The Lion, the Witch and the Wardrobe* was even more popular.

Key Symbol: The Stone Table

One of the mysterious prehistoric circles of giant stones in England is particularly famous: Stonehenge. C.S. Lewis visited that landmark in person, of course, and was impressed by it. Back then visitors could walk among the stones and touch them and sit on the low ones.

The stone that is lowest at Stonehenge is called the stone of sacrifice because people suspect that humans were bound and stabbed there in evil ceremonies thousands of years ago. There is no scientific basis for the story, supposedly, but it doesn't take much imagination to envision strange ceremonies taking place there. It is quite possible that humans were once sacrificed there, and it is almost certain that Stonehenge gave Lewis the idea of the Stone Table. (In "Accidental Magic," a story that Edith Nesbit published when Lewis was a boy, a ten-year-old named Quentin found himself alone at Stonehenge at nightfall; so he lay down on the altar stone and went to sleep. He awakened long ago when the ancient altar was brand new, and he almost ended up a human sacrifice.)

When death was defeated and Aslan came back to life, the stone table was split down the middle. The symbol of death turned into a symbol of new life. That reminds readers of the empty cross, the empty tomb and the torn curtain in the temple when Jesus was resurrected.

In later tales of Narnia, the location of the broken stone table becomes a memorial called Aslan's How (a hollow earthen mound). It is a place of solemn joy rather than a place of grief. So it was that when the Portland, Oregon, C.S. Lewis Society started publishing a newsletter that they named "The Chronicle," they placed a drawing of the broken stone table in the masthead as their symbol of Aslan's power.

The Lion, the Witch and the Wardrobe and the Bible

Isaiah 53:4–12 (RSV), foretelling the redemptive death of Christ, applies in part to the redemptive death of Aslan in this story. (The difference is that Aslan died in the story to save Edmund alone, not to save everyone.)

> Surely he has borne our griefs
> and carried our sorrows;
> yet we esteemed him stricken,
> smitten by God and afflicted.
> But he was wounded for our iniquities;
> upon him was the chastisement that made us whole,
> and with his stripes we are healed.
> All we like sheep have gone astray;
> we have turned every one to his own way;
> and the Lord has laid on him
> the iniquity of us all.
>
> He was oppressed and he was afflicted,
> yet he opened not his mouth;
> like a lamb that is led to the slaughter,
> and like a sheep that before its shearers is dumb,
> so he opened not his mouth.
> By oppression and judgment he was taken away;
> and as for his generation, who considered
> that he was cut off out of the land of the living,
> stricken for the transgression of my people?
> And they made his grave with the wicked
> and with a rich man in his death,

although he had done no violence,
and there was no deceit in his mouth.

Yet it was the will of the Lord to bruise him;
he has put him to grief;
when he makes himself an offering for sin,
he shall see his offspring, he shall prolong his days;
the will of the Lord shall prosper in his hand;
he shall see the fruit of the travail of his soul
    and be satisfied;
by his knowledge shall the righteous one, my servant,
make many to be accounted righteous;
and he shall bear their iniquities.
Therefore I will divide him a portion with the great,
and he shall divide the spoil with the strong;
because he poured out his soul to death,
and was numbered with the transgressors;
yet he bore the sin of many,
and made intercession for the transgressors.

Special Vocabulary in *The Lion, the Witch and the Wardrobe*

Efreets: afreets were demons or monsters of Mohammedan
    mythology
Ettins: giants
Hags: witches (now used for ugly old women)
Horrors: anything that causes horror
Incubuses: demons, especially those that bother sleeping people
Orknies: an orken was a monster or sea monster
Sprites: elves or goblins
Wooses: a woosel (from ouzel or ousel) meant a blackbird
Wraiths: spirits that can be seen

A Favorite Quotation in *The Lion, the Witch and the Wardrobe*

At the sound of his roar,
   sorrows will be no more . . .
And when he shakes his mane,
   we shall have spring again.

This is the message of *The Lion, the Witch and the Wardrobe*—for Edmund, for C.S. Lewis, for Lucy Barfield on the dedication page, and for all of us.

Favorite Food in *The Lion, the Witch and the Wardrobe*

Today Turkish Delight is just a pretty kind of candy. But at the beginning of this century a less innocent kind of Turkish Delight was popular with some university students in England. Their Turkish Delight was laced with hashish, and C.S. Lewis most likely had that in mind when he wrote about the witch's dangerous Turkish Delight that Edmund craved.

The Lion, the Witch and the Wardrobe has made Turkish Delight famous in the United States today. It might be hard to find in most candy stores, but it is available in little octagonal boxes from the Meltis Company, Bedford MK429PB, England ("Quality Confectionary for over 80 years, Original English Delicacies"). Two good American candies similar to Turkish Delight are called Applets and Cotlets. For better nutrition, however, one can snack upon sardines and toast, as served in a cave by a Faun. An old fashioned Christmas pudding, in season, will commemorate the coming of Father Christmas with his gifts. But most people would probably prefer "a gloriously sticky marmalade roll, steaming hot" with cups of tea, such as the Beavers served for dessert.

Here are two recipes for homemade Turkish Delight. The first is very complicated and the second is very easy.

Turkish Delight for Greedy Fools

Have 4 bowls ready. In the first one combine the grated rind and juice of 2 lemons and in the second one combine the grated rind and juice of 2 limes. In the third bowl combine the grated rind of 2 oranges and 1 grapefruit, the juice of 1 orange, 3 tablespoons of orange-flavored liqueur and 1 tablespoon lemon juice. In the fourth bowl combine 3 tablespoons *eau-de-vie de framboise* and 2 tablespoons each of raspberry syrup and lemon juice.

In a large heavy saucepan bring 2¼ cups water to a boil with ¼ teaspoon salt. Add 6 cups sugar, a little at a time, stirring constantly. Return mixture to a boil over moderate heat, stirring and washing down any sugar crystals clinging to the sides of the pan with a brush dipped in cold water. Reduce heat to moderately low and simmer the syrup, undisturbed, for 15 minutes. In a bowl sprinkle 10 envelopes (10 tablespoons) gelatin over 1½ cups cold water to soften for 5 minutes. Add the gelatin to the syrup, remove the pan from the heat and stir the mixture until the gelatin is dissolved. Divide the syrup among the 4 bowls.

Add food coloring to tint each mixture the desired shade of yellow, green, orange and pink. Rinse 4 loaf pans, 7½ by 3½ by 2 inches, with cold water and pour the flavored syrups into them. Sprinkle 3 tablespoons chopped walnut over the lemon mixture and 3 tablespoons sliced blanched pistachio nuts over the lime mixture. Let the syrups set at room temperature for at least 12 hours. Run a sharp knife around the sides of each pan and turn the candy out onto a smooth surface dusted with sifted powdered sugar. Dip the knife in cold water, cut the candy into squares or rectangles and roll the pieces in additional powdered sugar. Let the candy dry for 24 hours, coat it again with sifted powdered sugar and pack it in one layer in boxes lined with wax paper. Keeps about 1 week. Makes about 3¾ pounds.

Shortcut Turkish Delight for Little Victims

Dissolve 2 packages of unflavored gelatin in 1 cup of hot water. In another container dissolve 3 packages of flavored gelatin in 3 cups of hot water.

Combine these two solutions and pour them into a loaf pan so that the liquid is about ⅔ of an inch deep. Chill it in the refrigerator until it is very firm. Cut it into cubes and roll them in powdered sugar. Serve as soon as possible or the enchantment might fail.

When and Where in This Book

It is about 1940 in our world and Digory Kirk is now a professor in his fifties who owns a magic wardrobe. To his young visitors he seems to be a very old man because he has shaggy white hair and a white beard.

Following is a survey of the plot as it moves along from chapter to chapter:

1. Lucy accidentally found herself in Narnia.
2. After a visit with Mr. Tumnus the Faun, Lucy returned to England.
3. Edmund accidentally found himself in Narnia and met the "Queen of Narnia."
4. Edmund became addicted to magic candy.
5. Peter and Susan assumed that Lucy's Narnia was unreal and Edmund dishonestly agreed with them.
6. All four children found themselves in Narnia.
7. The four learned about Narnia while visiting Mr. and Mrs. Beaver there.
8. Edmund sneaked away to betray the others to the White Witch.
9. Edmund made his way to the Witch's castle and became a captive there.
10. As the children and the Beavers fled, Father Christmas arrived with his gifts.

11. The Witch discovered that her perpetual winter was beginning to thaw.

12. Aslan appeared, greeted his friends and knighted Peter.

13. The Witch demanded her right to kill Edmund.

14. Aslan gave himself to the Witch to die in Edmund's place.

15. Aslan came back to life.

16. Aslan revived all victims of the Witch who had turned to statues.

17. The children ruled Narnia for many happy years before returning to England.

Ten Facts That Add Meaning to This Book

1. *Pevensie.* The children's last name, Pevensie, is never mentioned in this book, but we learn it in the sequel. People suspect that Lewis chose that name because Pevensey Bay in England is the spot where the Normans landed in 1066 in the great invasion that changed England forever. The children themselves invade and change Narnia forever. But in another sense the last name of the children in this book is Adamson, because they are descended from Adam and Eve. Names and identities are extremely important in this story.

2. *Kirke and Macready.* The old professor's name is not given in this book, but it was Digory Kirke. (*Kirk* is a Scottish form of the word *church.*) It happens that when C.S. Lewis was in his teens he moved out into the lovely Surrey countryside to live with a retired white-haired teacher and his wife to prepare for his future university education. The teacher's name was William Kirkpatrick.

Professor Kirk's housekeeper named Mrs. Macready was an inside joke between C.S. Lewis and his brother Warren, because when they were little boys in Belfast their housekeeper's name was Mrs. McCreedy.

3. *Bigwardrobeinspareroom.* When Lewis was ten, E. Nesbit published "The Aunt and Amabel." In it there was a magic station between worlds called Bigwardrobeinspareroom (see Appendix One). Lewis's

Mr. Tumnus thought Lucy came from the city of War Drobe in the land of Spare Oom. It seems obvious where Lewis got that idea.

4. *Modesty.* Lewis had Mr. Beaver looking modest about the house he had built, as an author looks modest when you are reading a story he wrote. Lewis was poking fun at himself here, because he was saying this to everyone reading this story he wrote.

5. *Animal Characters.* Lewis quickly shows what the four children are like. Edmund's surliness and Peter's leadership appear on the second page. When the children think about exploring the nearby woods, each thinks of an appropriate animal. In the Macmillan (United States) edition Peter thinks first of eagles, stags and hawks; Lucy thinks of badgers; Edmund thinks of snakes; and Susan thinks of foxes. The girls will soon find themselves hunted like badgers and foxes. Peter exhibits chivalry and Edmund is justifiably called "a poisonous little beast."

6. *Fur.* From the beginning it is Lucy who savors the smell and feel of fur, not mean-spirited Edmund. Her enjoyment of the fur coats in the wardrobe not only leads her into Narnia, but also foreshadows her enjoyment of Aslan's fur.

7. *The Right Side.* The Faun's tearful decision to protect Lucy by risking himself in her place is the first dramatic act of moral choice and heroism in the book. It is followed by others, notably Peter's risky attack upon the wolf in an attempt to save Edmund, and Edmund's self-sacrifice in order to break the Witch's wand. Choice is a major theme in all of Lewis's fiction. Edmund complained, when he was still secretly siding with the Witch for his own gain, "Which *is* the right side?" But deep down he really knew. And eventually he was named "the Just" for his ability to know and do what is right.

8. *New Names.* Eventually Peter, who had thought of stags and falcons (in the Macmillan edition) and who received a grand sword and shield from Father Christmas, became a great warrior called King Peter the Magnificent. Susan, who had thought of foxes and who received an archery set and ivory horn from Father Christmas, became a gracious woman called Queen Susan the Gentle. Edmund, who had

once thought of snakes and whose costly gift was atonement from Aslan rather than something from Father Christmas, became a wise and quiet leader called King Edmund the Just. And Lucy, who had once thought of badgers and who received a dagger and healing elixir from Father Christmas, stayed cheerful and golden-haired (like Aslan) and was called Queen Lucy the Valiant.

9. *Father Christmas.* Lewis's good friend Roger Lancelyn Green strongly advised him to remove Father Christmas from the story, but he didn't. This part of the story was important to Lewis. He gave each of three good children one tool of offense and one tool of defense. Who is Father Christmas? (Like Aslan, he knows the children before he meets them.) Clearly, the Emperor over the Sea is like God the Father. Aslan is what Christ would be like in Narnia. Those who know the New Testament well enough know which member of the Trinity is the giver of spiritual gifts in our own world. It is the Holy Spirit.

10. *Dedication.* On a dedication page the art of writing and the art of living meet in a unique way. Lewis dedicated this book to Lucy Barfield, and one can't help suspecting that he named his heroine Lucy to please her.

"My dear Lucy," Lewis began, "I wrote this story for you, but when I began it I had not realized that girls grow quicker than books. As a result, you are already too old for fairy tales and by the time it is printed and bound you will be older still."

When I met her in 1975, Lucy's eyes twinkled as she told me "I think he must have understood me right from the start. He was a marvelous man."

"But some day you will be old enough to start reading fairy tales again," Lewis continued. "You can then take it down from some upper shelf, dust it and tell me what you think of it. I shall probably be too deaf to hear and too old to understand a word you say, but I shall still be your affectionate Godfather, C.S. Lewis."

There is irony here. C.S. Lewis did not live long after all. He died in 1963, when he was not quite 65 years old. And Lucy—a young ballet dancer, musician and teacher—was struck with paralysis (from the

White Witch's wand, in the form of multiple sclerosis) and unable to reach any upper shelves at all. Her long winter came early in life.

Lewis's promise has special meaning for Lucy Barfield and for every other reader also: "And when he shakes his mane, we shall have spring again."

Factual Quiz Just for Fun

1. The four children were named (a) Peter, Carol, Edmund, Lucy, (b) Edmund, Susan, Carol, Peter, (c) Robin, Edward, Susan, Lynn, (d) Susan, Edmund, Lucy, Peter.

2. Lucy entered Narnia through the Wardrobe (a) once, (b) twice, (c) three times, (d) four times.

3. The first person to risk his life for another in the story was (a) the old professor, (b) the Faun, (c) Aslan, (d) Giant Rumblebuffin.

4. "At the sound of his roar, _____ will be no more." (a) winter, (b) summer, (c) sorrows, (d) deep magic.

5. The name of the White Witch was (a) Jadis, (b) Lilith, (c) Wanda, (d) Wraithe.

6. The name of the castle on the sea with four thrones was (a) Pair Caravel, (b) Cair Paravel, (c) Cara Pirval, (d) Parra Ciravel, (e) Curve Parallel.

7. Edmund was *not* tempted by (a) greed for Turkish Delight, (b) desire to be a king, (c) desire to lord it over his brothers and sisters, (d) sexual desire.

8. Peter obeyed Aslan and risked his life killing the wolf in order to save (a) Edmund, (b) Susan, (c) Lucy, (d) the Faun.

9. Aslan died for the sins of (a) Adam, (b) all humankind, (c) Jadis, (d) Edmund.

10. The four kings and queens were finally led back to this world by a creature the Faun had told Lucy about on her first visit: (a) a talking robin, (b) a magic White Stag, (c) Mr. Beaver, (d) a Red Dwarf.

ANSWERS: 1 – d, 2 – c, 3 – b, 4 – c, 5 – a, 6 – b, 7 – d, 8 – b, 9 – d, 10 – b.

Thinking about Feelings

1. What is the most vivid scene in *The Lion, the Witch and the Wardrobe*? The most memorable? The most meaningful?

2. Does Aslan somehow change your feelings about Jesus? If so, can you say how?

3. With whom do you identify most in the story? Who or what do you love best?

4. What do you make of the idea that Aslan is wild, not a tame lion? How is that true of Christ?

5. Can we say "Aslan is on the move" today in our own world? Are we close to the Great Thaw here? How do you feel about this?

6. What were the causes of Edmund's downfall, according to the story and according to 1 John 2:16? ("For all that is in the world, the lust of the flesh and the lust of the eyes and the pride of life, is not of the Father but is of the world.") What was it in Edmund that enabled Aslan to win him over?

7. Lewis spent a whole paragraph telling about the mysterious effect that the unknown name of Aslan had on the four children the first time they heard it. For Edmund, under evil enchantment, the sudden feeling was terrifying horror. For Peter the chivalrous, the reaction was adventuresome bravery. For Susan, the lover of beauty, there was a reaction of delight. For cheerful and inquisitive Lucy, the youngest and purest of heart, the feeling was one of high expectation and vigorous freshness. The feelings seemed enormously meaningful, like feelings in certain dreams—"the dream so beautiful that you remember it all your life and are always wishing you could get into that dream again." This is Lewis's trademark, the longing for true joy or at least the longing for the longing for that joy. What does this longing really mean?

Benediction Based upon
The Lion, the Witch and the Wardrobe

May Aslan restore all names to their proper owners.
May the warmth of his breath come over us.
May his breath bring the stone parts of us to life.
May we live on both sides of the wardrobe door.

MIRAZ'
CASTLE

BOOK THREE

THE HORSE AND HIS BOY

The Main Theme: Slavery to Freedom

This is a story that begins with the hero knowing nothing but exploitation and oppression. He is treated like a slave. The main theme of the story is that of escaping to freedom. And the hero is not the only one doing so.

The freedom that is valued in this story is not irresponsible freedom; it is freedom which includes maturity, service and joy. If one is not ruled by high standards, love, and commitment, then one is ruled by whims, ambition, greed, lust or social pressure. A freedom without high values and self control is really just another kind of bondage.

With an escape into maturity, service, and joy one receives one's true identity. For Shasta that identity meant a high station which he did not particularly want. For Bree it meant being ordinary. So Shasta was freed from his low self-esteem and Bree was freed from conceit.

There are all kinds of slavery and all kinds of freedom. Inner slavery is even worse than outward slavery, and inner freedom is even better than outward freedom.

Another key theme in *The Horse and His Boy* is social class. The prince and the pauper theme never wears out. People love stories that show that the most important aristocracy of all is the aristocracy of merit. Lewis often contrasts arrogance with humility, political maneuvering with real leadership, the trappings of office with the purpose of the office.

Background of *The Horse and His Boy*

In 1945–1948 C.S. Lewis had a Middle Eastern student at Oxford named M.A. Manzalaoui, and Lewis supervised his thesis about eighteenth century English translations from Arabic. Mr. Manzalaoui has no doubt that Lewis reread the *Arabian Nights* to equip himself for that task, and it is obvious that before long Lewis drew on his familiarity with the *Arabian Nights* when he wrote *The Horse and His Boy*.

Lewis wrote *The Voyage of the "Dawn Treader," The Horse and His Boy* and *The Silver Chair* in 1950, but the publisher spread the books out and rearranged them. *The Voyage of the "Dawn Treader"* was published in 1952, *The Silver Chair* was published in 1953, and *The Horse and His Boy* was not published until 1954. That delay made *The Horse and His Boy* sixth to be published, although it was fourth to be written and third in the history of Narnia.

The Horse and His Boy had seven other titles before this one was chosen by the publisher. First Lewis called the book *Shasta and the North.* Then he tried *The Horse and the Boy.* He went on to *The Desert Road to Narnia, Cor of Archenland, The Horse Stole the Boy, Over the Border* and *The Horse Bree.*

Most readers don't notice that this book is dedicated to David and Douglas Gresham. Little did C.S. Lewis dream that he would end up giving these two boys vastly more than a book dedication. They were the sons of Joy Davidman Gresham, an American who moved to England to live near Lewis because his books, letters and friendship meant so much to her.

In 1957 Joy married Lewis, and in 1960 she died of cancer. In 1963 Lewis himself died. Joy's teen-age sons had lived at English boarding schools much of the time, but when Lewis died he kept his promise to Joy and left his literary estate to them. This meant that they would receive the royalties from all his books or that they could sell the literary estate to investors. They chose the latter course. Douglas has spent most of his life as a rancher and radio announcer in Australia; but by the time the Hollywood film *Shadowlands* made the Lewis marriage famous, he had moved to Ireland. David has reportedly lived in France, Israel and California. By the time *Shadowlands* was released, he had moved to India. Unlike Shasta and Cor, David and Douglas have never kept in touch.

Key Symbol: *Living Water*

There is a famous hymn called "Springs of Living Water."

When Shasta finally met Aslan ("No-one ever saw anything more terrible or beautiful"), he fell on his face before him. Aslan surrounded Shasta with his mane and its solemn fragrance, touched his forehead with his tongue, and looked into his eyes. Then in a swirling glory of light, he disappeared. But he left a mark.

There before Shasta in the grass was an extremely deep paw print (a sign of Aslan's power) which immediately became a spring, pouring forth a little stream that flowed downhill. Shasta drank and splashed his head with the beautiful water, as if in baptism. It was the beginning of a new day for him in more ways than one. Shasta's new relationship to Aslan is a bit like the message expressed in Isaiah 58:8–11 (TEV).

> Then my favor will shine on you like the morning sun and your wounds will be quickly healed. I will always be with you to save you; my presence will protect you on every side. When you pray, I will answer you. When you call to me, I will respond. If you put an end to oppression, to every gesture of contempt and to every evil word; if you give food to the hungry and satisfy those who are in need, then the dark-

ness around you will turn to the brightness of noon. And I will always guide you and satisfy you with good things. I will keep you strong and well. You will be like a garden that has plenty of water, like a spring of water that never goes dry.

The breaking forth of a new spring of water at a place of spiritual encounter is a traditional idea. Jesus spoke of it to the woman at the well as quoted in John 4:14 (TEV), ". . . whoever drinks the water that I will give him will never be thirsty again. The water that I will give him will become in him a spring which will provide him with life-giving water and give him eternal life."

Furthermore, Jesus stood up at the most important part of the Feast of Tabernacles in Jerusalem, at the water ceremony, and declared to the crowd, "Whoever is thirsty should come to me and drink. As the scripture says, 'Whoever believes in me, streams of life-giving water will pour out from his heart.'" John explains, "Jesus said this about the Spirit, which those who believed in him were going to receive. At that time the Spirit had not yet been given, because Jesus had not been raised to glory" (Jn 7:37–39).

The miraculous spring is a symbol of Christ's life in us.

The Horse and His Boy and the Bible

Part of the Old Testament book of the prophet Zechariah was apparently written in 520 B.C., urging the people of Jerusalem to rebuild the temple. Zechariah refers to Darius, king of Persia, who ruled over Judah at that time. For many Christians, Zechariah 9:9 is especially beloved because it seems to foretell Christ's entry into Jerusalem on a donkey 500 years later.

It is surprising to see the various ways that Zechariah can remind a reader of *The Horse and His Boy*. See Zechariah 1:7–11, 3, 4:6, 6:1–8, 7:8–10, 9:9, 9:12, 10:3–6, 13:1, 14:8, 14:20 (TEV).

In the second year that Darius was emperor, on the twenty-fourth day of the eleventh month (the month of She-bat), the Lord gave me a message in a vision at night. I saw an angel of the Lord riding a red horse. He had stopped among some myrtle trees in a valley and behind him were other horses—red, dappled and white. I asked him, "Sir, what do these horses mean?" He answered, "I will show you what they mean. The Lord sent them to go and inspect the earth." They reported to the angel: "We have been all over the world and have found that the whole world lies helpless and subdued."

In another vision the Lord showed me the High Priest Joshua standing before the angel of the Lord. And there beside Joshua stood Satan, ready to bring an accusation against him. The angel of the Lord said to Satan, "May the Lord condemn you, Satan! May the Lord, who loves Jerusalem, condemn you. This man is like a stick snatched from the fire." Joshua was standing there, wearing filthy clothes. The angel said to his heavenly attendants, "Take away the filthy clothes this man is wearing." Then he said to Joshua, "I have taken away your sin and will give you new clothes to wear." He commanded the attendants to put a clean turban on Joshua's head. They did so and then they put the new clothes on him while the angel of the Lord stood there. Then the angel told Joshua that the Lord Almighty had said: "If you obey my laws and perform the duties I have assigned you, then you will continue to be in charge of my Temple and its courts and I will hear your prayers, just as I hear the prayers of the angels who are in my presence. Listen then, Joshua, you who are High Priest; and listen, you fellow priests of his, you that are the sign of a good future I will reveal my servant, who is called The Branch! I am placing in front of Joshua a single stone with seven facets. I will engrave an inscription on it and in a single day I will take away the sin of this land. When that day comes, each of you will invite his neighbor to come and enjoy peace and security, surrounded by your vineyards and fig trees."

The angel told me to give Zerubbable this message from the Lord "You will succeed, not by military might or by your own strength, but by my Spirit. Obstacles as great as mountains will disappear before you. . . ."

I had another vision. This time I saw four chariots coming out from between two bronze mountains. The first chariot was pulled by red horses, the second by black horses, the third by white horses and the fourth by dappled horses. Then I asked the angel, "Sir, what do these chariots mean?" He answered, "These are the four winds; they have just come from the presence of the Lord of all the earth." The chariot pulled by the black horses was going north to Babylonia, the white horses were going to the west and the dappled horses were going to the country in the south. As the dappled horses came out, they were impatient to go and inspect the earth. The angel said, "Go and inspect the earth!"—and they did. Then the angel cried out to me, "The horses that went north to Babylonia have quieted the Lord's anger."

The Lord gave this message to Zechariah: "Long ago I gave these commands to my people: 'You must see that justice is done and must show kindness and mercy to one another. Do not oppress widows, orphans, foreigners who live among you, or anyone else in need. And do not plan ways of harming one another.'"

Rejoice, rejoice, people of Zion! Shout for joy, you people of Jerusalem! Look, your king is coming to you!

He comes triumphant and victorious, but humble and riding on a donkey—on a colt, the foal of a donkey.

The Lord says, "I am angry with those foreigners who rule my people and I am going to punish them. The people of Judah are mine and I, the Lord Almighty, will take care of them. They will be my powerful war-horses. From among them will come rulers, leaders and commanders to govern my people. The people of Judah will be victorious like soldiers who trample their enemies in the mud of the streets. They will fight because the Lord is with them and they will defeat even the enemy horsemen. I will make the people of Judah strong; I will rescue the people of Israel. I will have compassion on them and bring them all back home. . . ."

"When that time comes," says the Lord Almighty, "a fountain will be opened to purify the descendants of David and the people of Jerusalem from their sin. . . ."

When that day comes, fresh water will flow from Jerusalem, half of it to the Dead Sea and the other half to the Mediterranean. It will flow all year long, in the dry season as well as the wet.

At that time even the harness bells of the horses will be inscribed with the words: "Dedicated to the Lord."

Whether or not C.S. Lewis consciously had the book of Zechariah in mind when he wrote *The Horse and His Boy*, he must have had in mind Exodus and I Kings. When Shasta asked the Voice who he was, he answered "Myself" three times. The first time, the Voice was so deep the earth shook; the second time, the Voice was loud and clear; and the third time, the Voice was so soft you could hardly hear it. In Exodus 3:14 God answered Moses, "I am who I am." In I Kings 19:11–12 God spoke to Elijah in a wind, in an earthquake, in a fire and finally in a still, small voice.

Special Vocabulary in *The Horse and His Boy*

apophthegms: short, pithy, instructive sayings
bezzling: a misunderstanding of the word embezzling
cob: a short-legged, thick-set horse

copse: a small wood

downs: open, rolling country, with fairly smooth slopes usually covered with grass

estres: obsolete word meaning state of things or way of life

frowsty: musty, ill-smelling

furlong: an eighth of a mile

gooseberry fools, mulberry fools: British desserts made with fruit and cream

goosecap: obsolete word meaning booby, numskull and fool

hastilude: obsolete word for spear-play, a kind of tournament

heart's-scald: heart's burn (similar to heartache)

his suit was likely to be cold: his courtship was probably hopeless

manifest prognostics of indigestion: obvious signs of indigestion

pajock: rare and obscure old word meaning peacock

pasty: pastry

portcullis: a grating of iron or wooden bars or slats, suspended in the gateway of a fortified place and lowered to block passage

rum little creatures: odd, strange or queer little creatures

scapegoat: usually one who bears the blame for others; but, in this case, someone who has been off wandering alone

thymy: scented with thyme, a fragrant herb

we'll grease his oats: probably "we'll beat him." In American slang "grease" often means to bribe or rush.

weathercocks: weathervanes that turn with every shift of the wind

Vocabulary Detail: Jackals

Jackals are wild dogs of Asia and Africa which hunt in packs at night and were at one time believed to hunt prey for the lion. This old belief adds to the drama of the appearance of the Lion at the tombs where the jackals were.

When the word jackal is used for a human being it means one who does bad things for the benefit of someone else (like killing prey for a lion). In a story that occurs later in Narnia, *The Silver Chair*, there is such a jackal. Her name is Edith Jackle, and she pursues two English children into Narnia in her attempt to catch them for her friends, cruel school bullies.

What's in a Name?

There are meanings and associations connected with many of the names Lewis chooses in all his books, and sometimes they add to the story.

Aravis: This name looks like a variation of Avaris—the capital city of the Hyksos, a nomadic Semitic tribe from around Turkey that ruled Egypt in 1600 B.C. The Hyksos introduced horse-drawn chariots to Egypt.

Archenland: "Archen" is from the Greek language, and it suggests either ruler-land or olden-land. Either way, the *ch* is probably pronounced *k*, as in archangel.

Aslan: This is the Turkish word for lion. The surname Aslan is common enough to be listed in the telephone book of many metropolitan areas. There have been two prominent people named Aslan in recent decades. One was Dr. Ana Aslan of Romania, who was a well-known authority on the endocrine glands. (She claimed that laughter is good for those glands.) The other was Harry J. Aslan of Kingsburg, California who served in 1976–1977 as international president of the Lion's Club. When he learned about the triple coincidence from me, he was much amused. (In 1956 when I asked Lewis in person how to pronounce the name Aslan, he wouldn't say it for me; he insisted that people should pronounce it however they like. But in 1952 he had answered the question in a letter. "I pronounce it Ass-lan myself. And of course I meant the Lion of

Judah." He also explained that he had found this Turkish word when reading about *Arabian Nights*.

Calormen: "Calor" means heat in Latin, and "men" may possibly suggest menace as well as men. Calormen reminds us of the ancient empires of the Middle East, especially the Persian and Turkish empires.

Cor: This short name has two separate meanings which are appropriate. First is the English horn. (Cor responds to the different sounds of Calormene, Archenlandish and Narnian horns.) Second is heart.

Lune: In falconry, this word is a line for securing a hawk.

Narnia: Lewis's Narnia resembles medieval England, but in our world Narnia was once a hilltop colony twenty miles north of Rome. In 303 or 302 B.C. the Romans named it after the nearby Narnia River. This bit of history is recounted by E.T. Salmon in *Roman Colonization under the Republic* (London: Thames and Hudson, 1969).

Rabadash: This name suggests rabid and balderdash, as well as bad and dash.

Tash: In the Uzbek language of Central Asia tash means stone.

Tashbaan: Tashbaan closely resembles ancient Tashkent, the largest city in Central Asia and one of the oldest. It was established in a fruit-growing oasis on the Chirchik River in the midst of a vast desert. Through the centuries it has existed under Arabic rule, Turkish rule, Mongol rule, and the rule of the Soviet Union. When Lewis wrote *The Horse and His Boy*, Tashkent was populated by about a million Muslim or Communist Uzbeks and Russians. Before the fall of the Soviet Union in 1991, universal education in Russian was enforced, creating a very high rate of literacy. Lewis would no doubt have been amazed and delighted to hear that 40 years after he wrote *The Horse and His Boy*, there would finally be a few Christians working quietly behind the scenes in Tashkent, and the Chronicles of Narnia could be purchased there in Russian translation.

Tisroc: The roc is a fabulous bird of enormous size and strength in Arabian mythology. The Calormen ruler called Tisroc is supposedly descended from the great god Tash. Tash himself appears in *The Last Battle*, and indeed he is an enormous birdlike creature.

A Favorite Quotation in *The Horse and His Boy*

The following quotation must be important, because Aslan used almost the same words to both Shasta and Aravis at different times.

> "Child," he said, "I am telling you your story, not hers. No-one is told any story but their own."

Do you agree that we can grow in understanding of God's work in our own lives, but that we should be content not to be overly curious about God's work in other people's lives? Do you recall what Jesus said to Peter when Peter asked him about John's future? "...What is that to you? Follow me!" (Jn 21:22).

Favorite Food in *The Horse and His Boy*

The first meal mentioned in this book was a meat pasty (a small meat pie) with green cheese and dried figs—a typical Calormen sack lunch. Dried figs are an easy snack, if you can find some in a store. Later Shasta was given iced sherbet in Tashbaan to revive him from supposed sun stroke. Here sherbet means sweetened fruit juice mixed with water and ice, what we would call plain, pure fruit punch. Calormen also produced delicious melons and oranges, good to eat while reading this story.

Some people might like to celebrate *The Horse and His Boy* with a huge, rich, delicious dwarfs' breakfast: porridge and cream, bacon, eggs, mushrooms, buttered toast and coffee. But if you are health-conscious and adventuresome, buy a quart of goat's milk and try it so you will know what Aravis drank at the Hermit's house. Goat's milk is said to be better for humans than cow's milk.

When and Where of *The Horse and His Boy*

According to the chronology reportedly discovered after Lewis's death, this story takes place in 1940 English time and 1014 Narnian time. The four Pevensies have been ruling Narnia for fourteen years. (In 1015 they will hunt the White Stag and their reign will be ended.) Susan mentions the recent planting of an apple orchard at Cair Paravel; this will be recalled by Peter almost 1300 years later, Narnian time, in *Prince Caspian*.

According to this source, in the year 180 Prince Col of Narnia led some followers south and established the separate kingdom of Archenland. In 204 some Archenland outlaws fled south and established the separate kingdom of Calormen, which eventually became an empire. In 407 Olvin of Archenland killed the Giant Pire. In 1014 Prince Rabadash of Calormen was defeated when he attacked Archenland. In 1050 Ram the Great became king of Archenland after his father King Cor.

The Horse and His Boy is the only story of the seven Chronicles that does not involve anyone journeying out of our own world. On the map of Narnia locate Calormen, Tashbaan, the Hermit of the Southern March, Mt. Pire, Anvard, Stormness Head and Cair Paravel.

Facts and Ideas in *The Horse and His Boy*

1. Do you believe that Christ was (is) a real physical man, as Aslan is a real physical lion? Read John 20. Does Thomas remind you of Bree?

2. Who in the Old Testament was less wise than the talking animal he rode on? (Read the story of Balaam's ass in Numbers 22.)

3. What is the difference between Lasaraleen's preoccupation with clothes and the attention given to beautiful clothes by the Narnians and Archenlanders? Think about motives and character more than style.

4. How many plots and counter-plots can you locate in *The Horse and His Boy*? Did you notice that the disgraceful secret meeting of the

three highest leaders in Calormen (where the Tisroc betrayed his own son) is held right near the water-gate that Aravis is trying to reach? Would Lewis have eliminated the water-gate from his story if he had guessed that in less than twenty years after publication, the word Water-gate would become synonymous with high-level political scandal?

5. There is a major controversy about evidence that some of the posthumous writings published under C.S. Lewis's name (including a couple of Narnian fragments) are really forgeries. Did you notice that Lewis invented a fictitious forgery in *The Horse and His Boy*? (Aravis forged a letter to her father from Ahoshta.)

6. Why did Edmund look thoughtful when he said of Rabadash, ". . . even a traitor may mend. I have known one that did"?

Factual Quiz Just for Fun

1. Shasta was going to be sold by his father Arsheesh to (a) Tark-ish Anabaptist, (b) Aradudle Tisroc, (c) Tarkaan Anradin.

2. Shasta ran away with Bree, who was (a) a warhorse named Breehy-hinny-brinny-hoohy-ha, (b) a haystack, (c) a Narnian donkey.

3. Shasta and Bree were forced into journeying with Hwin and Aravis by (a) lack of food, (b) fear of lions, (c) fear of flying.

4. Calormen was (a) south of Archenland and Narnia, (b) between Archenland and Narnia, (c) westward (inland) from Narnia.

5. Prince Rabadash, son of the Tisroc, was determined to (a) capture Shasta, (b) marry Lasaraleen, (c) capture and marry Queen Susan.

6. The Narnians escaped (a) from Tashbaan in their ship "Spendour Hyaline," (b) from Archenland by fighting King Lune, (c) from Tarsus in their ship "The Dawn-Treader."

7. The Hermit of the Southern March (a) had lived 70 years and never seen Aslan, (b) had lived 901 years and could foretell the future, (c) had lived 109 years and had never met Luck.

8. Shasta "accidentally" crossed the mountain Stormness Head, thus summoning (a) Narnians to save Anvard, (b) an aardvark to marry Ahoshta, (c) the Raven Sallowpad to Mount Pire.

9. Shasta had been kidnapped as a baby by (a) Arsheesh, (b) Lord Bar, (c) Corin Thunder-Fist.

10. Rabadash was permanently pacified by (a) becoming a horse, (b) becoming a donkey, (c) growing an extremely long nose.

ANSWERS: 1 – c, 2 – a, 3 – b, 4 – a, 5 – c, 6 – a, 7 – c, 8 – a, 9 – b, 10 – b.

Thinking about Feelings

Good Luck, Bad Luck and No Luck At All

When Aravis said it was luck that the Lion only gave her long shallow scratches, the Hermit replied that he did not believe in Luck. What did he mean?

A little later, heartsick Shasta said he was the unluckiest person in the whole world, and then he told his sorrows to his unseen and unwanted companion in the dark.

"I do not call you unfortunate," was the answer. Shasta asked if it was not bad luck to meet so many lions. After that he learned who his companion really was and forgot his self-pity.

If you have suffered severe unresolved trials and sorrows in your own life, imagine yourself in Shasta's place telling Jesus what bad luck you have had. Then imagine Jesus answering, "I do not call you unfortunate," and assuring you that he has been watching over you in love through all the hardships. (And real hardships they were, of course.) Are pain and hurt easier to bear when one feels loved?

This is very much like the Christian practice of the "healing of memories," in which old wounds are soothed or healed by vivid realization that Christ's active love was quietly present during harmful past experiences.

Four Questions about Feelings

1. How do you feel about the idea that if you do one good deed your reward is usually to be set to do another and harder and better

one? Does that fact make you cringe? Do you find it exciting or depressing?

2. With which character in this story did you identify most closely? What was the best thing that happened to that character?

3. How do you feel about Lewis's obvious admiration for females who are active and athletic and brave?

4. Two girls in this story escaped forced marriages. Would you rather marry someone well-to-do who does not meet your character standards, or stay single and risk loneliness? Cor and Aravis eventually married, but never stopped quarreling and making up. For you, would lots of quarreling and making up make a marriage more interesting or more tiring?

Creative Responses to *The Horse And His Boy*

1. The following poem was written by Ian McMurdo of Leicestershire, England.

Aslan

Do not look behind you, Man-child.
The stir in your hair
Is a lion. The fur of one paw
Covers your continent.

Dare you raise your head? His mane
Has might in its mass;
And a halo, a white solar fringe,
Crowns him as conqueror.

Look down. His tawny back
Supports Your feet. No such beast,
Wild or circus, would meet such mundane
Needs, roaring contentment.

Does this poem speak of Shasta? Does it speak of you?

2. "Paws for Thought" was the first and only album by a group in England called "Aslan." Their album cover featured Aslan, his paw print, and the broken stone table.

3. "On the Road to Narnia" was the motto on the colored T-shirts of 120 high schoolers who went on the road for a week in the summer of 1976. Instead of heading north across the desert of Calormen on horses, they headed south along the coast of California on bicycles. It was the carefully planned project of a Sacramento church. The caravan of a dozen groups of ten, spread out over ten miles of road, cycled from Santa Maria to Anaheim, using Narnian stories as their theme each weary evening. Los Angeles served as their dangerous Tashbaan, but they survived it intact and were featured on television when they arrived at their destination—Disneyland. After a few days at Disneyland they flew home, reportedly taking something of Narnia home with them—religious commitments, increased friendship and leadership, and a sense of community.

Benediction Based upon *The Horse And His Boy*

We are aliens in this land and we don't know it.
Chase us and guide us to our true country.
We don't know the way or the real reasons.
We are still rude and ragged, but you love us.
Bring us safe to our Father-King at last.

BOOK FOUR

PRINCE CASPIAN

The Main Theme: Fasting to Feasting

This is a story that begins with too little to eat. As soon as the children realized that they had been pulled away by magic into another land (perhaps Narnia) instead of completing their journey back to school, they started to wonder about food.

"This isn't going to be such fun," Peter worried.

He was right. Much of the adventure wasn't fun. And much of the time the children had to get by on apples, water, and then the meat of a dangerous bear they eventually butchered. But the dreary diet was replaced by joyful feasts in the end.

First came the sunrise feast in chapter 11. Aslan started it with a giant roar, awakening the entire land. After a while marvelous vines and bunches of grapes were everywhere. And a marvelous bunch of partying people right out of Greek mythology were everywhere also. Bacchus and his crew would have been dangerous if this had not been Aslan's good and wholesome celebration. (Dionysus is another name for Bacchus, and Dionysian revels is the term used for wild, uninhibited parties.) Where do fun and celebration really belong?

In chapter 14 this party resumes the next morning as a "moving feast" that spreads joy. As the feast moves, both nature and society are set right along the way. Some of Christ's New Testament miracles are reflected in Chapter 14.

In Chapter 15 the wonderful sunset victory feast continued until it turned into a fireside slumber party. All night Aslan and the moon gazed at each other with joyful and unblinking eyes while the guests at the feast slept, full and happy and safe. Aslan's friends, unlike the Telmarines, love woods and animals and running water.

Think about *plans* as another main theme in *Prince Caspian*: Plans in delay . . . Plans in disarray . . . Plans A and Plans B . . . Plans that fail . . . Plans that prevail . . . The Great Planner.

Background of *Prince Caspian*

C.S. Lewis expected to write only one tale of Narnia, *The Lion, the Witch and the Wardrobe*. But as soon as he finished that in 1949 he wrote *Prince Caspian*. It poured out of him. *Prince Caspian* was published in 1951.

Prince Caspian begins with exactly the same words as *The Lion, The Witch And The Wardrobe*, "Once there were four children whose names were Peter, Susan, Edmund and Lucy . . ." But two-thirds of the way through the book when Lucy said, "I thought you'd come roaring in and frighten all the enemies away—like last time," Aslan answered that things never happen the same way twice. Is that true in the Bible? How about in our own lives?

Lewis's first title for *Prince Caspian* was *Drawn into Narnia*. His publisher did not like it. His second title was *A Horn in Narnia*. His publisher did not like that one either. So then Lewis suggested *Prince Caspian*, with its subtitle *The Return to Narnia*. Most people never notice the subtitle. Except for that forgotten subtitle, not one of the Narnian Chronicles has the word Narnia in its title.

Lewis once remarked that *Prince Caspian* was the least popular of his Narnian Chronicles. Can you account for that?

The Key Symbol: A Door in the Air

The Door in the Air idea may have originated in a strange dream that C.S. Lewis recorded in his diary in 1923 when he was not a Christian. He was sitting on the bridge at his college at dusk. Then he walked up a hill with a group of people and at the top he saw a window in the air. There a lamb was slain and spoke with the voice of a human. The dream was a mystery to Lewis and seemed like a nightmare, but in retrospect it can be interpreted as a symbol of his future acceptance of Christianity.

In *Prince Caspian* the Door in the Air is a mystery. It will appear again in the next Narnian Chronicle, *The Voyage of the "Dawn Treader"*. In both cases, it is an image of the passageway between involvement in our world and in God's higher reality. Humans do not control the door.

Lewis's Door in the Air has been used on the covers of two albums of Christian music. First was Bob Hurd's album "O Let Him In," with a photo of a door standing alone in the countryside. Second was Bob Ayala's album "Joy by Surprise." Inside are photos of Ayala, who is blind, with his eyes hidden by dark glasses. The back of the album shows Bob's back as he walks into a doorway with a beautiful scene of Narnia visible ahead of him. The front of the album is a front view of Ayala as he approaches Aslan from the Door in the Air. He doesn't have on dark glasses anymore. He can see.

There are other junctions in the Narnian stories. In *The Lion, the Witch and the Wardrobe* the children got to Narnia through a wardrobe closet. But the Professor warned them not to try to use the same route twice. In *Prince Caspian* they went through a train station. Trains and stations are powerful symbols.

When C.S. Lewis had just turned 24, he wrote in his journal that he dreamed that he was in a station waiting room and found a children's story by Edith Nesbit that he had not read before. He became so interested in the fantasy story that he missed his train. Lewis used a train station again in *The Last Battle*.

Prince Caspian and the Bible

Psalm 148 (RSV) relates to *Prince Caspian* in several ways. Look for key words they have in common. Look also for the key truth they have in common.

> Praise the Lord!
> Praise the Lord from the heavens,
> praise him in the heights!
> Praise him, all his angels,
> praise him, all his host!
> Praise him, sun and moon,
> praise him, all you shining stars!
> Praise him, you highest heavens,
> and you waters above the heavens!
> Let them praise the name of the Lord!
> For he commanded and they were created.
> And he established them forever and ever;
> he fixed their bounds which cannot be passed.
> Praise the Lord from the earth,
> you sea monsters and all deeps,
> fire and hail, snow and frost,
> stormy wind fulfilling his command!
> Mountains and all hills,
> fruit trees and all cedars!
> Beasts and all cattle,
> creeping things and flying birds!
> Kings of earth and all peoples,
> princes and all rulers of the earth!
> Young men and maidens together,
> old men and children!
> Let them praise the name of the Lord,
> for his name alone is exalted;
> his glory is above earth and heaven.

He has raised up a horn for his people,
praise for all his saints,
for the people of Israel who are near to him.
Praise the Lord!

Special Vocabulary in *Prince Caspian*

grandcestors: Caspian's mistaken word for ancestors
how or howe: a variation of the word hollow, usually meaning small
    valley, used in Scotland and northern England
Jinn: a kind of spirit in Islamic mythology, also known as a genie
mazer: a large metal or wooden drinking bowl or cup
theorbo: an obsolete stringed instrument
torch: British for flashlight

This Book's Minor Characters

Arivir: the morning star
Belisar, Uvilas, the Passarids, Arlian, Erimon: lords murdered circa 2290
Bromios, Bassareus, the Ram: names for the classical god Dionysus
Bulgies: the bears
Camillow: the Hare
Clodsley Shovel: the Mole (Lewis found this real man's name in naval
    history.)
Destrier: Caspian's horse
Glenstorm: the Centaur
Glozelle and Sopespian: two of Miraz's lords
Gwendolyn: a history pupil
Hardbiters: more badgers
Hogglestock: the Hedgehog
King Miraz and Queen Prunaprismia: Caspian's evil uncle and aunt
    who reigned from 2290 to 2303
King Nain of Archenland: in the Urdu language in India, *nain* means
    the eye

Lilygloves: chief mole in Narnia between 1000 and 1015
Mentius, Obentinus, Dumnus, Voluns, Voltinus, Girbius, Nimienus,
  Nausus, Oscuns: the Fauns
Miss Prizzle: a bad history teacher
Nikabrik: a sour Black Dwarf
Old Raven of Ravenscaur: Scaur means a rocky place or cliff
Pattertwig: a squirrel
Pomely: Glozelle's horse
Pomona: Roman goddess of fruit trees
Reepicheep: a Talking Mouse
Rhindon: Peter's sword
Ship, Hammer and Leopard: three Narnian constellations
Silenus: forest god of classical mythology
Splendour Hyaline: the royal ship
Tarva and Alambil: two planets of Narnia, for victory and peace
Trufflehunter: a Badger
Wimbleweather: the Giant

A Favorite Quotation in *Prince Caspian*

> You came from the Lord Adam and the Lady Eve. And that
> is both honour enough to erect the head of the poorest beg-
> gar and shame enough to bow the shoulders of the greatest
> emperor on earth.

How does the Bible explain this mixture of honor and shame?

Favorite Food in *Prince Caspian*

While enjoying *Prince Caspian* people might enjoy "large
yellowish-golden apples as firm and juicy as you could wish to see."
Or "really good grapes, firm and tight on the outside, but bursting
into cool sweetness when you put them into your mouth." Or one
could go all out and serve "peaches, nectarines, pomegranates, pears,

grapes, strawberries, raspberries—pyramids and cataracts of fruit." But plain apples alone would suffice. Barbecued bear is quite another matter.

Words You Wouldn't Want to Eat

The cheeks of the dark Telmarine soldiers became the color of cold gravy when they saw Aslan. Try to think of a better description. (It's no use.)

When Lewis was ten years old he wrote in his diary, "We had enormous helpings of boiled beef with thick, sickening yellow fat and little grey puddings known as slime balls." Lewis's mother had died and he was living in a small boarding school run by a truly cruel, insane man. "He was a big, bearded man with full lips like an Assyrian king on a monument, immensely strong, physically dirty."

Lewis described how this headmaster (school principal) was always beating one poor boy in particular, a very good boy. He beat him relentlessly for making a mistake in geometry. The boy had become a trained sufferer, "and no sound escaped him until, toward the end of the torture, there came a noise quite unlike a human utterance. That peculiar croaking or rattling cry, that and the gray faces of all the other boys and their deathlike stillness, are among the memories I could willingly dispense with." Fear is gray.

King Miraz, who aimed to control young Caspian's education and then aimed to murder him, seems to be a reflection of Lewis's first headmaster.

On a lighter note, when Lewis was seventeen and living very happily with his excellent private tutor, Mr. Kirkpatrick, he reflected wistfully, "If only they would dust the butter, it would be quite ideal . . ."

When, Where and How Long

When

1. In *The Lion, the Witch and the Wardrobe* Peter was thirteen, Susan was twelve, Edmund was ten and Lucy was eight.

2. One year has passed in England and it is 1941 there.

3. In Narnia 1303 years have passed while one year passed in England.

Where

Trace all the journeys in this book on the map of Narnia. Locate:
1. Aslan's How
2. Lantern Waste
3. Cair Paravel
4. Beruna

How Long

1. Chapters 1–3: Arrival in Narnia
2. Chapters 4–7: The dwarf's story
3. Chapters 8–11: The long journey
4. Chapters 12–14: Accomplishing the task
5. Chapter 15: Rewards

This book goes on and on. Some think the first eleven chapters are too long. Did the children in the story think that part of their adventure was too long?

Prince Caspian and Education

Prince Caspian emphasizes education more than any of the other Chronicles, although education is part of all seven. Try to name all the different sets of teachers and pupils in *Prince Caspian*, starting with the old lady and the little prince.

Lewis's first "teacher" was his own beloved nurse (a full-time mother's helper), who told him Irish fairy tales when he was little. Later he had a governess (a home teacher hired by his parents) named Miss Harper. He wrote in his diary, "She is fairly nice for a governess, but all of them are the same." He had just turned nine.

Except for his period as a soldier in World War I, Lewis was a student and then a teacher his entire life, until his final illness. Yet in 1951 he remarked a bit ruefully, "I think the educational world is rather anti-me." Do most people feel occasionally that the "world is rather anti-me"?

What happened to each of the good and bad teachers and pupils in *Prince Caspian*?

In a sense, the best teacher of all in the Narnian Chronicles is Aslan himself. Consider the lessons that he is teaching in *Prince Caspian* and the other books. Here he tells Lucy that every year she grows, she will find him bigger. Is it true that as we grow, we find God bigger? How can that be?

Factual Quiz Just for Fun

1. In this book the children enter Narnia from (a) a wardrobe, (b) a church door, (c) a seat in a railway station, (d) an orchard.

2. The reason they didn't recognize their old home was that (a) it was so splendid, (b) it was in ruins, (c) they had forgotten it.

3. Peter's sword was named (a) Rhindon, (b) Caspian, (c) Fenris Ulf, (d) Destrier.

4. Doctor Cornelius was *not* (a) Caspian's tutor, (b) part dwarf, (c) a rebel against Miraz, (d) a real Telmarine.

5. The mysterious hollow mound built centuries ago over the Stone Table is called (a) Aslan's Who, (b) Miraz's Why, (c) Caspian's Where, (d) Aslan's How.

6. Which is *not* one of the three key magical places in Narnia? (a) the Stone Table, (b) Lantern Waste, (c) Telmar, (d) Cair Paravel.

7. Much of this story is told by (a) Trumpkin, (b) Nikabrik, (c) Caspian, (d) King Peter.

8. Who received special guidance from Aslan and failed to follow it? (a) Peter, (b) Edmund, (c) Susan, (d) Lucy.

9. The formal duel between Peter and Miraz did *not* end in (a) murder, (b) a draw, (c) general battle, (d) a forest alive and rushing to the river.

10. The children returned to England through (a) a blast on the horn, (b) the Wardrobe, (c) a door in the air, (d) a long hike.

ANSWERS: 1 – c, 2 – b, 3 – a, 4 – d, 5 – d, 6 – c, 7 – a, 8 – d, 9 – b, 10 – c.

Thinking about Feelings

1. "If you had felt yourself sufficient, it would have been a proof that you were not," Aslan told Caspian when he made him king. What is the difference between humility and false guilt? Between healthy self-esteem and foolish pride?

2. Imagine yourself burying your face in "the living and strokable gold of Aslan's mane." How does that make you feel about Aslan? About Christ?

3. When the old lady said joyfully, "I've been waiting for this all my life. Have you come to take me away?" Aslan said, "Not on the long journey yet." How do you honestly feel about being taken away on that long journey to the afterlife? Do you ever feel that you are waiting to look into Christ's face?

4. The little old woman at death's door said, "Eh, you've done something to our well. That makes a nice change, that does," and she jumped out of bed! This is reminiscent of Jesus changing water to wine at the wedding in Cana. Do you think that Christ ever does something to people's wells today? (A well is sometimes a symbol for the deep inner mind.)

5. Aslan told Susan, "You have listened to fears." Are wrong moves often the result of fears? Be specific as you consider how this works in your own life. Think also of how the verse 1 John 4:18 ("There is no fear in love, but perfect love casts out fear. For fear has to do with punishment and he who fears is not perfected in love") works out in *Prince Caspian*.

Prince Caspian as Inspiration

One of the subjects that Dr. Cornelius taught Caspian was "versification." Reading and writing poetry was one of Lewis's lifelong loves.

In fact, his early ambition was to be a great poet. One summer when an American named Mary Stolzenbach was traveling in a camper, she taped a large poster of Aslan on the ceiling so that when she lay down she could look up at him. This is a poem that came to her.

Star Over Narnia

So clear and silver-shrill, aloft and far
High over Narnia sings a star,
"Come bow, come bow
Now to the Lion's love!"

He sings above, and far below
In Lantern Waste a light will glow;
Young fauns will sit in spellbound row
To hear a tale of long ago.

And in Cair Paravel tonight,
The wine is poured, the fires are bright,
The feast is kept, and rulers great
Sit in their strong and holy state,
But all, like Lucy, with laughing heart
(For she has chosen the better part)—

Now meet the rough embrace,
Now see the shining face
Of Lion's love.

Father of Aslan, Emperor over Sea,
Send us, us too, a light,
Here where our earth falls deeper into night,
A light from thee.

Para-Ecology

Parapsychology means beyond regular psychology. One can coin the word para-ecology to mean beyond ordinary ecology. Lewis was an ardent nature-lover, and his fictitious tree-hood (like Tolkien's) goes far beyond that of the Sierra Club. In Chapter 9 the trees seemed to stir. In Chapter 10 Lucy caught them dancing. In Chapter 11 the woods moved cross-country. In Chapter 14 the woods chased the evil army away. In Chapter 15 the trees celebrated and feasted. (Trees will also play an important part in *The Last Battle*.)

When Lewis had the woods in *Prince Caspian* move cross-country and help defeat the evil forces, he was intentionally echoing a scene in Shakespeare's *Macbeth*. In *Prince Caspian* he was also echoing the spirit of Isaiah 55:12: "You will go out in joy and be led forth in peace; the mountains and hills will burst into song before you and all the trees of the field will clap their hands" (NIV).

Sidney Lanier's poem "A Ballad of Trees and the Master" strikes such deep chords in many readers that some cannot read it aloud without tears. It echoes an ancient Anglo-Saxon devotional story, "The Dream of the Rood," in which the tree that was used as the cross tells of its love for Christ.

A Ballad of Trees and the Master

> Into the woods my Master went,
> Clean forspent, forspent.
> Into the woods my Master came,
> Forspent with love and shame.
>
> But the olives they were not blind to him,
> The little gray leaves were kind to him
> The thorn tree had a mind to him
> When into the woods he came.
>
> Out of the woods my Master went,
> And he was well content.
> Out of the woods my Master came,
> Content with death and shame.

When Death and Shame would woo him last,
From under the trees they drew him last;
'Twas on a tree they slew him last
When out of the woods he came.

Benediction Based upon *Prince Caspian*

Give me patience when I get tired of my day-to-day diet of life.
Give me the courage to follow your leading,
   even when it makes me unpopular.
Let me always learn and teach with integrity.
Give me a foretaste of joy in the victory feast.
Give me the grace to walk bravely, when my time comes,
   through your Door in the Air.

BOOK FIVE

THE VOYAGE OF THE "DAWN TREADER"

The Main Theme: West to East

This is the story of a journey to the East, the direction that traditionally meant "God-ward." In fact, east is the first direction mentioned in the Bible (Gen 2:8), and the traditional design for churches had the altar at the east end of the nave. The first book C.S. Lewis wrote after his conversion, *The Pilgrim's Regress*, is about a young man who did all he could to "go west," away from God, toward an island paradise. He finally learned that because the world is round, his distant island in the west was really the Eastern Mountains he had feared, the land of God. In contrast, in *The Voyage of the "Dawn Treader"* Reepicheep longs to reach the land of God in the east.

Do you ever think of your entire life as a journey? The most famous and beloved of all books on this theme is *The Pilgrim's Progress* written by John Bunyan in about 1670. It is said that for over two centuries most homes in England had two books if no others—the King James Bible and *Pilgrim's Progress*, two of the finest works of English literature. The first was perfected by a committee of brilliant scholars, and the second was written by a poor uneducated country man in his jail cell. C.S. Lewis loved them both.

"The journey to truth and light must first cross the ocean within." "Life is a journey, not a destination." Like many inspirational sayings, these are elastic enough to convey both truth and error.

The Biblical theme of a journey to the Promised Land has sustained many people through this life. The journey to the Utter East in the third Chronicle of Narnia sustains people also. In a sense, *The Voyage of the "Dawn Treader"* takes its place next to the Bible and *The Pilgrim's Progress* as one of the great guides for the human journey.

Background of *The Voyage of the "Dawn Treader"*

In 1919, when he was 20 years old, C.S. Lewis published his first book, called *Spirits in Bondage*. He had recently recovered from wounds he suffered in France in World War I, and now he was an ambitious student at Oxford. *Spirits in Bondage* contains 40 of the poems he wrote in his late teens expressing his anti-Christian view of life. (As he reflected later, he was quite angry at God for not existing.)

Ironically, the prologue he wrote for that book ends with lines that sound like a foretaste of *The Voyage of the "Dawn Treader"*:

> In my coracle of verses
> I will sing of lands unknown. . . .
> Sing about the Hidden Country fresh
> and full of quiet green.
> Sailing over seas uncharted to a port
> that none has seen.

Twelve years later Lewis became a Christian. After another 20 years he wrote the story of Reepicheep sailing away in his coracle. Many readers would say that Lewis found his "Hidden Country."

On August 16, 1949, the year before he published *The Voyage of the "Dawn Treader,"* Lewis wrote to a correspondent:

"I should think I *do* like salt water and in all its forms; from a walk on the beach in winter when there is not a soul in sight, or seen washing past (rather like beaten copper) from the deck of a ship, or knocking one head over heels in great green ginger-beer-coloured waves. I grew up close to it, but there's no chance of getting there now. On the other hand I have discovered the joys of shallow river bathing. . . . It is like bathing in *light* rather than in water; and having walked for miles, you can *drink* it at the same time" (*Letters of C.S. Lewis*, Harcourt, Brace & World, 1966; p. 218).

There is no question that C.S. Lewis put his own life and his own dreams (good and bad) into this book. On May 29, 1954, Lewis answered a letter from a fifth grade class in Maryland about *The Lion, the Witch and the Wardrobe; Prince Caspian* and *The Voyage of the "Dawn Treader."* He told them there would be seven books altogether and that number four, *The Silver Chair*, was already out. Reepicheep and Nick-i-brick don't represent anything in our world. "But of course anyone in our world who devotes his whole life to seeking Heaven will be *like* Reepicheep and anyone who wants some worldly thing so badly that he is ready to use wicked means to get it will likely behave like Nick-i-brick. Yes, Reepicheep did get to Aslan's country." He ended his letter by saying, "The only way for us to [get to] Aslan's country is through death, as far as I know; perhaps some very good people get just a tiny glimpse before then. Best love to you all. When you say your prayers sometimes ask God to bless me" (*C.S. Lewis, Letters to Children*, Macmillan, 1985; p. 45).

The Key Symbol: A Magic Spell

The forgotten story in the Magic Book was a spell "for the refreshment of the spirit." It was three pages long and the story and pictures became real to Lucy. It was the loveliest story she ever read, but it faded away like a dream. It was about a cup, a sword, a tree and a green hill.

Not everyone who reads *The Voyage of the "Dawn Treader"* realizes that Lucy has discovered the story of redemption. Some people suspect that, but can't understand it completely. The cup seems to be the cup of the Last Supper, and the sword may be the sword Peter used in his misguided attempt to defend Jesus in the Garden of Gethsemane or the sword that pierced Jesus in the side. The tree is the cross upon which Christ was crucified. But what is the green hill?

Exactly 50 years before C.S. Lewis was born in Belfast, a 30-year-old Irish woman named Cecil Francis (Fanny) Alexander looked at the green hill outside that city (now covered with ordinary city sprawl) and imagined the hill of Calvary outside Jerusalem. Then she wrote what became a favorite Good Friday hymn:

> There is a green hill far away
> Outside a city wall
> Where the dear Lord was crucified
> Who died to save us all.

Lewis almost surely heard that hymn repeatedly in his childhood in the Belfast church where his grandfather was the preacher. (Fanny Alexander wrote other beloved hymns also, among them: "All Things Bright and Beautiful," "Once in David's Royal City," and "Jesus Calls Us O'er the Tumult.")

After reading in the Magic Book, Lucy completed her task and Aslan appeared. He promised Lucy he would tell her the magic story for years and years. As he sent the children home later and Lucy asked him how to get into his country from our world, he answered, "I shall be telling you all the time." Of all good stories, the best we ever read or hear is the story that is "for refreshment of the spirit" indeed!

The Voyage of the "Dawn Treader" and the Bible

There are several ways in which the strangely beautiful passage of prophecy Ezekiel 43:2–4, 47:1–12 (RSV) relates to *The Voyage of the "Dawn Treader"*:

And behold, the glory of the God of Israel came from the east; and the sound of his coming was like the sound of many waters; and the earth shone with his glory. And the vision I saw was like the vision which I had seen when he came to destroy the city and like the vision which I had seen by the river Chebar; and I fell upon my face. As the glory of the Lord entered the temple by the gate facing east, the Spirit lifted me up and brought me into the inner court; and behold, the glory of the Lord filled the temple. . . .

Then he brought me back to the door of the temple; and behold, water was issuing from below the threshold of the temple toward the east (for the temple faced east); and the water was flowing down from below the south end of the threshold of the temple, south of the altar. Then he brought me out by way of the north gate and led me round on the outside to the outer gate, that faces toward the east; and the water was coming out on the south side.

Going on eastward with a line in his hand, the man measured a thousand cubits and then led me through the water; and it was ankle-deep. Again he measured a thousand and led me through the water; and it was knee-deep. Again he measured a thousand and led me through the water; and it was up to the loins. Again he measured a thousand and it was a river that I could not pass through, for the water had risen; it was deep enough to swim in, a river that could not be passed through. And he said to me, "Son of man, have you seen this?"

Then he led me back along the bank of the river. As I went back, I saw upon the bank of the river many trees on the one side and on the other. And he said to me, "This water flows toward the eastern region and goes down into the Arabah; and when it enters the stagnant waters of the sea, the water will become fresh. And wherever the river goes every living creature which swarms will live and there will be very many fish; for this water goes there, that the waters of the sea may become fresh; so everything will live where the river goes. Fishermen will stand beside the sea; from Engedi to Eneglaim it will be a place for the spreading of nets; its fish will be of very many kinds, like the fish of the Great Sea. But its swamps and marshes will not become fresh; they are to be left for salt. And on the banks, on both sides of the river, there will grow all kinds of trees for food. Their leaves will not wither nor their fruit fail, but they will bear fresh fruit every month, because the water for them flows from the sanctuary. Their fruit will be for food and their leaves for healing."

Special Vocabulary in *The Voyage of the "Dawn Treader"*

action: a legal case

Bottom: a foolish man in Shakespeare's play *A Midsummer Night's Dream*

carracks: galleons of the 15th and 16th centuries

catches: fragments of songs

cheek: impudence

cogs: medieval single-masted merchant ships

coracle: a small basket-like Welsh boat covered with skins

crescent: $1.50 (fictitious)

dromonds: large fast-sailing vessels of the Middle Ages

Isle of Wight: a half-hour ferry ride from the south coast of England

minim: about 2¢ (fictitious)

pike: a shafted weapon with a sharp head

poltroon: coward

postern: a back door

pound: about $3.00 when Lewis wrote this book

Queen Mary: great Cunard (British) ocean liner, now on display in Long Beach, California

saloon: a dining room or leisure room on a ship

swank: showing off

trice: a moment

Vocabulary Detail

Eustace's rhyme: "Some kids who played games about Narnia/Got gradually balmier and balmier" isn't even an assonance (similar sound) in the United States. It sounds much better in England, where *Narnia* and *balmier* sound much alike. *Balmier* and *barmier* also sound much alike there. *Barmy* and *barmier* are real words; they mean frothy—from *barm*, which is brewer's yeast formed on ale while it is fermenting. (A British phrase for mentally unbalanced is "barmy in the crumpet.") Evidently the British used to say *barmy* to mean bubble-brained and, because it sounded like *balmy*, they spelled it both ways and still do. In the United States it is spelled and pronounced balmy, and few realize that it relates to fermentation froth rather than fair weather!

A Favorite Quotation in *The Voyage of the "Dawn Treader"*

> "I will not tell you how long or short the way will be; only that it lies across a river. But do not fear that, for I am the great Bridge Builder. . . . But there I have another name. You must learn to know me by that name. This was the very reason you were brought to Narnia, that by knowing me here for a little, you may know me better there."

What is the river and who the Bridge Builder? Does the last sentence apply to all Narnia readers?

Favorite Food in *The Voyage of the "Dawn Treader"*

While enjoying *The Voyage of the "Dawn Treader,"* one might like to drink bottled mineral water, especially a kind that is naturally carbonated. Peacocks are impractical, along with boars' heads, sides of venison and pies shaped like elephants. For a one o'clock lunch Lucy had a magic omelette with cold lamb, green peas and strawberry ice cream—very English. Roast fish would also be ideal. In any event, readers may be glad they don't have to eat dead dragon flesh as Edmund did.

When, Where and Who in This Book

2306–2307: Narnian dates of the voyage (when Caspian was 16).
1942: the year of Edmund, Lucy and Eustace's voyage (when they were 12, 10 and 9).
August 6: the day the three children joined the voyage.
August 22–September 2: the storm.
September 3–11: limping east in bad condition.
September 11–17: on Dragon Island.

Although this story starts in Cambridge, England, and ends there, so much happens in the meantime that an overview is helpful. There are ten main parts of the voyage.

1. The 400-league journey from Cair Paravel to the four western islands, taking 30 days.
2. The Lone Islands adventures at Felimath, where the voyagers were captured by slave traders, and at Doorn, where they cleansed the corrupt government at Narrowhaven.
3. Twelve days in a great storm followed by eight days of anxiety.
4. A week on Dragon Island and a brief stop at Burnt Island.
5. Five days at sea and a deadly struggle with a Sea Serpent.
6. Escaping the evil spell of Deathwater Island.
7. The Island of the Voices and the Magic Book, where Coriakin ruled.
8. The Dark Island, where nightmares came true.
9. Ramandu's Island, where Aslan's table was spread with food.
10. To the World's End, where the sky joins the earth.

Caspian set out on this voyage to find seven lost lords (victims of Miraz) first mentioned in *Prince Caspian*. Here is what he found:

1. Lord Bern: became duke of the Lone Islands
2. Lord Octesian: apparently killed by the dragon
3. Lord Restimar: turned to a gold statue
4. Lord Rhoop: saved from the Dark Island
5. Lord Revilian: saved from enchanted sleep
6. Lord Argoz: saved from enchanted sleep
7. Lord Mavramorn: saved from enchanted sleep

Aslan appears seven different times in this book:

1. Aslan appeared to Eustace and transformed him.
2. Aslan walked by and broke the spell of greed at Goldwater Island.
3. Aslan appeared in the Magic Book to save Lucy from temptation.
4. Aslan came to Lucy when she made hidden things visible.
5. As a bright albatross Aslan led the ship from the dark island.
6. The lion's head on the wall came to life and directed Caspian.
7. The Lamb became Aslan.

Facts and Ideas Related to This Book

1. Why did Eustace lie on his side after Reepicheep taught him some manners?

2. The overturning of Governor Gumpas' table reminds some readers of a passage in the Gospels (check Mt 21:12 and Mk 11:15). Ramandu's "fire berries" remind some of a passage in the Old Testament (check Is 6).

3. Many people liken Eustace's dragon form to his selfish, stupid inner nature, and his stripping to salvation. How perfect was Eustace after his transformation? Lewis said, "It would be nice, and fairly nearly true, to say that 'from that time forth Eustace was a different boy.' To be strictly accurate, he began to be a different boy. He had relaps-

es." (In Edith Nesbit's story "The Cat-hood of Maurice," a boy was turned into the cat he had tormented. "If you have ever been a cat you will understand something of what Maurice endured." When he became a boy again after a week of misery, Nesbit said, "Please dismiss any fears which you may entertain that after this Maurice became a model boy. He didn't. But he was much nicer than before.")

4. Aslan told Lucy that she had made him visible. "Do you think I wouldn't obey my own rules?" What kind of laws does God obey? What kind does God overrule?

5. When Edmund said that things aren't always what they seem, Ramandu's daughter answered, "You can't know," referring to her good intentions. "You can only believe or not." Do Christians have to make a leap of faith? Belief-choice will be vividly portrayed in the final scene with the Green Lady in *The Silver Chair*.

6. In 1977 the Committee for Urban Ministries in Paterson, New Jersey, founded an inner-city school and named it "The Dawn Treader School." A Presbyterian campground in California had already taken Narnia as its name.

7. American Mary Stolzenbach, who was living in the Far East, once wrote to a friend in the States: "Would you believe a Narnia group in Japan? Saw their announcement, all in Japanese. They meet in a room at Rikkyo, the university supported by the Japanese Episcopal Church and they're called *Na-ni-a-koku monogatari dokusha-kai*— literally, 'society of readers of the tales of the country of Narnia.'"

8. When Reepicheep left his sword standing in the Sea of Lilies and sailed away alone, he was re-enacting what King Arthur did at the end of his life. Lewis knew that. In fact, he mentioned King Arthur early in this book, as if to hint that Arthur's nobility would be echoed in this story.

Factual Quiz Just for Fun

1. Eustace Clarence Scrubb was the Pevensies' (a) cousin in Cambridge, (b) friend in Oxford, (c) nephew in Narnia.

2. Eustace, Lucy and Edmund entered Narnia through (a) a door in the sky, (b) a wardrobe, (c) a picture of a ship.

3. Caspian was looking for (a) revenge against Miraz, (b) the World's End, (c) seven friends of his murdered father.

4. The evil that Lord Bern helped the voyagers destroy in the Lone Islands was (a) a magic curse, (b) slavery, (c) evil dreams.

5. After leaving the Lone Islands, the "Dawn Treader" suffered two weeks of (a) storm and drifting, (b) attacks from sea serpents, (c) captivity.

6. Dragon Island is where (a) Eustace's cure began, (b) Eustace became perfect, (c) Eustace was condemned.

7. Deathwater Island is where (a) gold means death, (b) Lord Restimore became rich, (c) all water was poison.

8. On the Island of the Voices (a) coracles are called monopods, (b) monopods are called Dufflepuds, (c) Dufflepuns are called monopuds.

9. The Dark Island was (a) made light by Caspian, (b) where dreams come true, (c) where Aslan was seen as a Lamb.

10. Ramandu was (a) a retired star with a lovely daughter, (b) a magician, (c) a lost lord.

ANSWERS: 1 – a, 2 – c, 3 – c, 4 – b, 5 – a, 6 – a, 7 – a, 8 – b, 9 – b, 10 – a.

Thinking about Feelings

1. Aslan told Lucy: "I call all times soon." How do you feel about that as you look at your own life: past, present and future?

2. The first sentence of this book has been quoted in a collection of unusual first sentences: "There was a boy called Eustace Clarence Scrubb, and he almost deserved it." (Lewis probably chose the name Eustace in memory of a spoiled brat named Eustace Robinson in E.M. Forster's "The Story of a Panic" in *The Celestial Omnibus" and Other Stories* [1911], according to scholar Douglas Loney.) Clive Staples Lewis chose the nickname Jacksie when he was four years old and

remained Jack to close friends and relatives all his life. To other acquaintances he went by Lewis or Mr. Lewis. How do you feel about your own name? How have you handled it? Do you hope that the Bible is factual when it says that God has a new name for each of us?

3. On the first page of *The Voyage of the "Dawn Treader*," Lewis wrote frankly, "Eustace Clarence disliked his cousins . . ." They were forced to spend summer vacation at his house, without their parents. (On the first page of Edith Nesbit's story "The Related Muff," the narrator began by saying, "We had never seen our cousin Sidney till that Christmas Eve, and we didn't want to see him then, and we didn't like him when we did see him." Sidney was forced to spend Christmas vacation at their house, without his parents.) What kind of "unfriendly cousins" may await many of us in life?

4. Have you ever experienced any horror in your life, asleep or awake, as terrible as those at the Dark Island? Do you think that in your own dark hours this chapter with its message "Courage, dear heart" could help? It has been of help to some who were suffering.

5. How do you feel about Christ represented as a lion? As a lamb? The Southern California C.S. Lewis Society chose the Lion and Lamb image from *The Voyage of the "Dawn Treader"* as their emblem for the masthead of their journal "The Lamp-Post." Artist Tim Kirk drew it for them.

The Voyage of the "Dawn Treader" as Inspiration

Joe R. Christopher, author of *C.S. Lewis* in the Twayne Series of English authors, wrote the following poem as a blessing to follow the christening of a baby girl in the Episcopal Church.

Lullaby

Now sleep, my daughter, sleep awhile—
    the mystic rites are done
    your imagination to love is won,

no sinful thoughts defile—
how short we stay with thoughts so well!
before we fall as Eve once fell;
yet through this moment's glory,
we know the happy ending's story.

So dream, my daughter, dream awhile—
of twyform centaurs good,
of satyrs dancing quite unrude
with dryads free from guile,
of knights who need no sword nor targe,
of monopods and lions large,
of lambs in pastures leaping,
and mystic spears nor yet ableeding.

When wake, my daughter, as wake you must,
and all the world's awry,
when you've no language but a cry,
remember what has passed:
the golden dreams are far more real
than all the pain our days reveal,
so learn the dreams of foy—
and find them true in after-joy.

(*Foy* ordinarily means feast, but here it also refers to faith.)

Do you believe that infants can be blessed by God in their dreams? Do you believe that the golden dreams in the Chronicles are in an eternal sense more real than the pain in our lives and that we will "find them true in after-joy"?

Benediction Based upon *The Voyage of the "Dawn Treader"*

Lord of the Utter East, you know where each of us is on this
 life voyage.
Please preserve us from Deathwater curses and Dark Island
 dreams.
Give us the courage to endure through rough storms and dull
 calms.
Keep telling us how to get to your country from our world.
And help us to know you better here.

BOOK SIX

THE SILVER CHAIR

The Main Theme: Darkness to Light

Moving from dullness or darkness into light happens over and over in *The Silver Chair*. In this book, as in Biblical imagery, love and light and truth go together. In *The Silver Chair* evil power that works against life is expressed in a dull autumn day, black armor and horse, dark places, grey light, dim drowsy radiance, a pitch black voice, and sooty blackness. (It must be remembered that Lewis was not implying that all dwellers in darkness are evil; the great white owl Glimfeather is good, and the Earthmen are good. And Lewis was hardly prejudiced against the color black; he described himself as black-haired.)

God's good power is expressed first in sunset light, then in things glittering, silver or golden. There is winter sunshine, silver mail, the morning sun, the bright skies of Overland, and sunlit lands. When the children find themselves in the place where a shed drop of Aslan's blood could raise one of his old friends from the dead—"suddenly they were standing in a great brightness of mid-summer sunshine."

The Silver Chair could well serve as a book-length illustration of 1 John 1:7, 2:3 (TEV): "If we walk in the light, as he is in the light, we have fellowship with one another, and the blood of Jesus, his Son, purifies us from all sin. . . . We know that we have come to know him if we obey his commands."

The Silver Chair is about learning to obey God, even when it means plunging into dark places to do his will.

Background of *The Silver Chair*

Lewis's first title for this book was *The Wild Waste Lands.* When the publisher did not like that, he tried *Night under Narnia, Gnomes under Narnia, News under Narnia* and finally *The Silver Chair.*

Anyone who likes the underworld parts of *The Silver Chair,* with gnomes burrowing under the earth, would probably enjoy *The Princess and the Goblin* by George MacDonald. This was a great favorite of C.S. Lewis himself. Lewis only discovered *The Princess and the Goblin* and its sequel *The Princess and Curdie* in his 20s, although they were written long before he was born. There is no question that *The Princess and the Goblin* influenced Lewis when he wrote *The Silver Chair.* Lewis reread the *Princess* books shortly before he became a Christian. They are extraordinary adventure stories with spiritual meaning. Lewis later wrote that George MacDonald taught him more than any other writer and was the single largest influence in his becoming a Christian.

In his autobiography *Surprised by Joy,* Lewis tells about the many mistakes he made before he became a Christian: "What I like about experience is that it is such an honest thing. You may take any number of wrong turnings; but keep your eyes open and you will not be allowed to go very far before the warning signs appear. You may have deceived yourself, but experience is not trying to deceive you. The universe rings true wherever you fairly test it."

Some readers find that *The Silver Chair* helps them to cope with their wrong turnings and the accidents that befall them in life. As Puddleglum declared, "There are no accidents. Our guide is Aslan." This assurance tallies with Joseph's triumphant conclusion in Genesis 50 (after decades of cruel misfortunes) that God can use evil for good.

Key Symbol: A Shield of Faith

So long as Rilian was enchanted and held captive by the Queen of Underland, his shield was black and had no design on it. But when the Queen (witch) was destroyed and Underland was freed, Rilian's shield turned the color of silver with a brilliant red lion on it—the Lion. In the Bible the shield is a symbol of faith in God. In Ephesians 6:16 Paul said, ". . . above all, taking the shield of faith, with which you can quench all the flaming darts of the evil one."

As soon as he showed his new shield to his friends, Rilian said "This signifies that Aslan will be our good lord, whether he means us to live or die." He had each of his friends kneel and kiss the picture of Aslan on his shield and then set out in confidence, knowing that they were in great danger. In the course of their journey, when at last they seemed to be permanently trapped in the dark, Rilian repeated his assurance, "Courage, friends. Whether we live or die Aslan will be our good lord." That is the shield of faith.

The following prayer translated from Irish of the eighth century seems to express Prince Rilian's faith perfectly:

> Be thou my vision, O Lord of my heart;
> Naught be all else to me save what thou art.
> Thou my best thought, by day or by night,
> Waking or sleeping thy presence my light.
>
> Be thou my wisdom, thou my true word;
> I ever with thee, thou with me, Lord.
> Thou my great Father, I thy true Son,
> Thou in me dwelling and I with thee one.
>
> Be thou my battle-shield, sword for the fight;
> Be thou my dignity, thou my delight,
> Thou my soul's shelter, thou my high tower.
> Raise thou me heavenward, O power of my power.

Riches I heed not, nor man's empty praise,
Thou mine inheritance, now and always;
Thou and thou only, first in my heart,
High King of heaven, my treasure thou art.

High King of heaven, after victory won,
May I reach heaven's joys, O bright heaven's sun!
Heart of my own heart, whatever befall,
Still be my vision, O, ruler of all.

The Silver Chair and the Bible

Again Jesus spoke to them, saying, "I am the light of the
world; he who follows me will not walk in darkness, but will
have the light of life." The Pharisees then said to him, "You
are bearing witness to yourself; your testimony is not true."

Jesus answered, "Even if I do bear witness to myself, my
testimony is true, for I know whence I have come and whith-
er I am going, but you do not know whence I come or whith-
er I am going. You judge according to the flesh, I judge no
one. Yet even if I do judge, my judgment is true, for it is not
I alone that judge, but I and he who sent me. In your law it is
written that the testimony of two men is true; I bear witness
to myself, and the Father who sent me bears witness to me."

They said to him therefore, "Where is your Father?" Jesus
answered, "You know neither me nor my Father; if you knew
me, you would know my Father also." These words he spoke
in the treasury, as he taught in the temple; but no one arrest-
ed him, because his hour had not yet come. Again he said to
them, "I go away, and you will seek me and die in your sin;
where I am going, you cannot come."

Then said the Jews, "Will he kill himself, since he says,
'Where I am going, you cannot come'?" He said to them,
"You are from below, I am from above; you are of this world,

I am not of this world. I told you that you would die in your sins, for you will die in your sins unless you believe that I am he."

They said to him, "Who are you?" Jesus said to them, "Even what I have told you from the beginning. I have much to say about you and much to judge; but he who sent me is true, and I declare to the world what I have heard from him." They did not understand that he spoke to them of the Father. So Jesus said, "When you have lifted up the Son of man, then you will know that I am he, and that I do nothing on my own authority but speak thus as the Father taught me. And he who sent me is with me; he has not left me alone, for I always do what is pleasing to him." As he spoke thus, many believed in him.

Jesus then said to the Jews who had believed in him, "If you continue in my word, you are truly my disciples, and you will know the truth, and the truth will make you free" (Jn 8:12–32 RSV).

This passage relates to *The Silver Chair* in several ways. Did the Green Lady die in her sins? Did Aslan leave the children alone after sending them on their way? How was it that continuing in the word of Aslan enabled the children to know the truth and to be set free? How do these religious principles work out in real life?

Let no one deceive you with empty words, for it is because of these things that the wrath of God comes upon the sons of disobedience. Therefore do not associate with them, for once you were darkness, but now you are light in the Lord; walk as children of light (for the fruit of light is found in all that is good and right and true), and try to learn what is pleasing to the Lord. Take no part in the unfruitful works of darkness, but instead expose them. For it is a shame even to speak of the things that they do in secret; but when anything is exposed by the light it becomes visible, for anything that becomes visible is light. Therefore it is said, "Awake, O sleeper, and arise from the dead, and Christ shall give you light." Look carefully then how you walk, not as unwise men but as wise, making the most of the time, because the days are evil. Therefore do not be foolish, but understand what the will of the Lord is (Eph 5:6–17).

There are several ways in which this passage relates to *The Silver Chair*. Do you ever feel that our days are evil and that there are forces at work in our world undermining God's Kingdom? Is it possible for Christians to be deceived by empty words? To be foolish? Think of two characters in *The Silver Chair* who were in a sense sleepers who were awakened and raised into the light. Do you believe that Christ awakens both kinds of sleepers (the enchanted and the dead) today?

Narnia in the Bible: The Bible in Narnia

The Silver Chair is the third Narnian book specifically to mention the Bible in passing, as if by accident. At the beginning of *The Lion, the Witch and the Wardrobe* Lewis remarks that some of the books in the old professor's house were bigger than a Bible in a church. In the magician's library in *The Voyage of the "Dawn Treader"* Lucy found that some books were bigger than any church Bible you have ever seen. And in *The Silver Chair* we realize that Bibles are not used at all at the bad school called Experiment House because no one there has heard of Adam and Eve.

Furthermore, *The Silver Chair* seems to be strongly influenced by one particular Bible passage, Isaiah 57:13–16 ". . . he who takes refuge in me shall possess the land, and shall inherit my holy mountain. And it shall be said, 'Build up, build up, prepare the way, remove every obstruction from my people's way.' For thus says the high and lofty One who inhabits eternity, whose name is Holy 'I dwell in the high and holy place, and also with him who is of a contrite and humble spirit, to revive the spirit of the humble, and to revive the heart of the contrite. For I will not contend forever, nor will I always be angry' . . ."

It is easy to see this passage in the scene where Aslan tells the contrite Jill, "I will not always be scolding," and then takes her to his high and holy Mountain.

Special Vocabulary in *The Silver Chair*

ark: box
blamey: rare slang, equivalent of "darned"
buffers: shock absorbing devices on railroad tracks
cairn: pile of stones
caraways seeds: used for cooking and medicine
cock-a-leekie soup: Scottish chicken broth with chopped leeks (like onions)
cock-shies: the game of throwing things at a target
coil: noisy disturbance
comfits: candied fruit
Ettinsmoor: ettins is an obsolete word for giants and a moor is open wasteland
Fie on gravity!: Down with serious behavior!
funk: schoolboy slang for coward
fusty: musty
goods: trains, freight trains
Head: principal (short for headmaster or headmistress)
hols: school vacation (short for holidays)
kirtle: woman's loose gown worn in the Middle Ages
marches: border country
parliament of owls: Lewis's pun, referring to *Parliament of Fowls* (which sounds practically the same), a medieval writing by Chaucer
poppet: affectionate term for a child
portcullis: iron grating in a gateway
possets: drinks rather like hot spiked eggnogs, for head colds
puttees: ankle-to-knee leg coverings

queues: waiting lines, especially common in World War II
ration books: World War II sets of coupons required for purchases
riding crop: whip
slit in a pillar box: slot in a mail box
squib: firecracker
strait: confined

A Favorite Quotation in *The Silver Chair*

"Even in this world it is the stupidest children who are
the most childish and the stupidest grown-ups who are most
grown-up."

What adult qualities are desirable in children, and what childlike
qualities are desirable in adults? Are you taking the best of your childhood qualities with you clear through adulthood? Is it ever too late
for an adult to develop more curiosity, transparency, fun, wonder,
warmth, playfulness and awareness of feelings?

Favorite Food in *The Silver Chair*

Early in *The Silver Chair* the children were at a great dinner. Later in
the story they almost *were* a great dinner, along with their stringy, mud-
flavored friend—who was good at cooking eel stew.

The easiest snack for readers of *The Silver Chair* would be a few peppermint candies such as the one Eustace gave Jill.

A dwarfish midnight breakfast consists of sausages, potatoes, hot
chocolate and baked apples. For anyone with a microwave oven, whole
baked apples are quick and easy. Cut out part of the core and put in
a bit of brown sugar, butter, cinnamon and a few raisins. Place apples
on a baking dish and allow about three minutes per apple, plus five
minutes of residual heat after the oven goes off.

When and Where in *The Silver Chair*

How Time Flies

This story evidently takes place in 2356 in Narnia and 1942 in England. (*The Voyage of the "Dawn Treader"* took place in 2306–7.) Caspian the Seafarer married Ramandu's daughter in 2310, at age 20. Prince Rilian was not born until 2325, when his father Caspian the Seafarer was 35. Caspian lost his wife and his son Rilian when he was 55 and Rilian was 20. When this story takes place Rilian is a youthful 31 and Caspian is an aged 66. Eustace figures that 70 years have passed since he last saw Caspian, but in fact only 50 years have passed. Is this Eustace's mistake or Lewis's? It seems excusable either way.

Where Things Are

Find the River Shribble on your map and trace the rest of the journey as you imagine it.

London in Narnia

The Silver Chair refers to three of the most famous landmarks in England: Stonehenge, St. Paul's Cathedral and Trafalgar Square. The latter two are in London and are visited by many people who have read *The Silver Chair*. Lewis says that the giants' bridge soared as high as the dome of St. Paul's Cathedral. That is high indeed, because St. Paul's (circa. 1700) boasts one of the greatest domes in the world. Trafalgar Square, in the heart of London, is an immense open space full of people, pigeons and fountains. When Jill first saw Aslan he was lying before her just like the lions in Trafalgar Square. There are four lions there, facing four directions, at the foot of the column honoring Admiral Nelson.

Lewis's first visit to London, with his mother when he was a very little boy, included a visit to these famous lions. His mother wrote, "Jacks is delighted with Trafalgar Square." She also noted that nothing in London impressed him more than the mice at the London Zoo. Lewis liked mice the rest of his life.

169

Facts and Ideas Concerning *The Silver Chair*

Morphology: the Study of Shapes and Forms

The Silver Chair emphasizes shapes and forms. In the field of biology, morphology is the study of forms and structures of plants and animals. Lewis included vivid examples of biological morphology in *The Silver Chair*, ranging from giants and gnomes to grotesque varieties of earthmen.

An "ectomorph" is a tall, thin person, and Puddleglum is an extreme ectomorph. An "endomorph" is a round, fat type of person, and Trumpkin is an extreme endomorph. *The Silver Chair* also contrasts the Green Lady taking a terrible new form and King Caspian taking a wonderful new form.

Geomorphology means the study of characteristics, origin and development of land forms. *The Silver Chair* includes dramatic geomorphic features such as underground caverns and an earthquake.

Thanatology: the Study of Death

The Silver Chair emphasizes death. For example, funerals were mentioned twice in passing before the children found themselves bereaved. Puddleglum remarked that one advantage of starving underground was that it would save on the cost of a funeral. Jill told Puddleglum that although he sounded as doleful as a funeral, he was really happy. And the last thing he got to say to her was, "Now, speaking of funerals ..." That happy scene foreshadowed the pathos of Caspian's death only two pages later when the solemn, triumphant music of the king's return was changed into wailing strings and disconsolate blowing of horns and a tune to break your heart.

That funeral music was heard clear up on the Mountain of Aslan and Aslan himself wept over the body of King Caspian. Thanks to the blood of Aslan, Caspian was more than restored. This is reminiscent of Jesus weeping over the death of his friend Lazarus before he called him forth from the grave to new life. Although Lewis believed in life after death, he, too, grieved intensely when he lost loved ones to death. He said that people probably need to weep more than they do.

Epistemology: the Study of Knowing

Epistemology is the study of how we can know what we know. It is one of the three main branches of philosophy. (C.S. Lewis was in his youth a professor of philosophy.) The scene with the Green Witch where she challenged the children's knowledge and almost overcame them with her "reasoning" is real epistemology in dramatic form. (Philosophy professor Robert Hurd says her epistemology is "worthy of Feuerbach, Nietzsche, Marx and Freud.")

Robert Hurd makes two observations about the Witch's argumentation. First, it is such a powerful line of thought that it is in a sense "bewitching." However it does not in fact prove anything. The witch pretends to prove the nonexistence of Aslan, when in fact she bases her case upon assuming at the start that he and his world do not exist. She also pretends that the children have come to believe in the reality of the Overworld because of wishful thinking. That claim happens to be untrue, but it is also irrelevant. Finally Puddleglum's realistic answer shifts the argument to practical ground.

Speculations or accusations about a believer's state of mind don't begin to disprove the beliefs themselves. Such speculations don't tell us anything about ultimate reality. Lewis warns us not to be fooled that way.

Factual Quiz Just for Fun

1. Eustace Scrubb and Jill Pole got to Aslan's country through (a) a picture of a ship, (b) a door in a school wall, (c) a railroad station.

2. The first sign Aslan gave Jill was (a) Eustace must greet his old friend as soon as he arrives in Narnia, (b) Jill must drink from a stream, (c) Eustace must save Jill from falling.

3. The children do not soon meet (a) Trumpkin, a deaf old dwarf, (b) Glimfeather, a large white owl, (c) Caspian, the old king whose son is lost.

4. The children's guide and helper was (a) Respectowiggle the Marshglum, (b) Puddlesquirm the Swamp-glum, (c) Puddleglum the Marshwiggle.

5. The second sign of Aslan was (a) to travel north to the ruined city of ancient giants, (b) to travel north to the giants' castle, (c) to seek a beautiful lady.

6. The third sign of Aslan was (a) to obey the writing on a stone, (b) to obey the writing in a cookbook, (c) to attend a feast.

7. At the House of Harfang Aslan showed the travelers the message (a) BEWARE, (b) PLAY DUMB, (c) UNDER ME.

8. Mullugutnerum was (a) an Earthman in Underland, (b) Queen of the Deep Realm, (c) Warden of Overworlders.

9. The fourth sign of Aslan was (a) the lost prince was dressed in black, (b) the lost prince might be insane, (c) the lost prince would ask a favor in the name of Aslan.

10. Which is false? (a) Jill emerged into a snow dance, (b) King Caspian was restored to youth and health, (c) Prince Rilian became king of Narnia, (d) Jill and Eustace returned to school alone, as they had left.

ANSWERS: 1 – b, 2 – a, 3 – c, 4 – c, 5 – a, 6 – a, 7 – c, 8 – a, 9 – c, 10 – d.

Thinking about Feelings

1. Do you have any phobias such as an undue fear of heights (Eustace), dark underground places (Jill), open spaces (Golg) or insects (Lucy and C.S. Lewis)? Are you sensitive to such phobias in other people or do they irritate you?

2. How do you feel about Aslan's words: "You would not have called to me unless I had been calling to you"? Do you believe that you might sometimes be affected by Christ's love and concern when you don't consciously feel his presence or love at all? Once Lewis went for a haircut when he did not intend to do so, and it turned out that his barber had been praying that he would come in because he needed to see Lewis. Do you feel that God directs you?

3. Do you find it much harder to endure trials when you expected pleasure instead?

4. How do you feel about the claim that there is nothing like a good shock of pain for dissolving certain kinds of magic (delusions about life)? Is there a danger in a life of comfort and peace and prosperity?

5. Pessimistic Puddleglum welcomes adversity in hopes of improving his character, which is flawed (he thinks) by excessive optimism and cheer. C.S. Lewis, who loved the novels of Charles Dickens, is no doubt having fun here with his memory of a delightful character named Mark Tapley in Dickens' comic novel *Martin Chuzzlewit*. The remarkably cheerful Mark Tapley welcomes adversity as eagerly as Puddleglum in hopes of improving his character, which is flawed (he thinks) by a tendency toward gloom. Lewis seriously advised readers that it is our duty to be as cheerful as we can. How do his Narnian Chronicles realistically encourage readers not to despair?

6. What do you think Aslan meant when he said he has swallowed boys and girls, kingdoms and realms? What did he mean when he said you will die of thirst if you don't come near him, because there are no other streams?

7. Do you believe that God has ever given people important messages in their dreams? Why or why not? If he has done it in the past, do you think that he would ever do it now?

8. Do you think, as Lewis did, that evil powers (Northern Witches) come to us in very different forms at different times to trick us? Are you trickable?

9. The following is a common attack on the Christian faith: "You've had a father, and so you imagined a bigger and better father and called him God. 'Tis a pretty make-believe. There is no God, no spiritual reality, no heaven or hell. Give up those childish dreams." Does this bewitching argument intimidate you?

The Silver Chair as Inspiration

Lewis has tried to whet the appetite of readers for the next book to be published. (*The Horse And His Boy* was sixth to be published, although it was fourth to be written and third in the history of Narnia.) After the magnificent banquet that the children enjoyed at Cair Paravel at the beginning of *The Silver Chair*, "a blind poet came forward and struck up the grand old tale of Prince Cor and Aravis and the horse Bree, which is called *The Horse and His Boy* and tells of an adventure that happened in Narnia and Calormen and the lands between, in the Golden Age when Peter was High King in Cair Paravel. (I haven't time to tell it now, though it is well worth hearing.)" Then when Rilian made his dangerous journey away from Underland, whistling and singing, what he sang was "snatches of an old song about Corin Thunder-fist of Archenland."

This is like an invitation from Lewis for someone to write part of *The Horse and His Boy* in poetry, and for someone to write a song about Corin Thunder-fist. The following verse follows neither of those suggestions, but it reviews in rhyme some of the key transitions in *The Silver Chair.*

The Silver Chair

Out of the depths, onto the height;
Out of the loss, into delight.

Out of the lies, into the facts;
Out of the bonds, into the acts.

Out of the doubts, into belief;
Out of the torment, into relief.

Out of the error, into the truth;
Out of the grave, back into youth.

Out of temptation, into correction;
Out of regrets, into perfection.

Out of the gloom, into the sun;
Out of the doom, into the fun.

Out of the evil, into the right;
Out of the darkness, into the light.

Benediction Based upon *The Silver Chair*

Lord of the Real Sun,
Help me to remember my signs.
Deliver me from the many Houses of Harfang
    in this world.
Show me how to tell sanity from insanity.
Give me the courage to break enchantments,
    even when it hurts.
And bring me at last to your holy mountain
      where life is renewed.

BOOK SEVEN

THE LAST BATTLE

The Main Theme: Death to Life

Many people prefer not to think about their own future death. Some hope to live on in their descendants; others hope to live on in their creative works, their contributions to society or their reputations and human remembrance. How long can any of those things themselves survive death?

As C.S. Lewis says elsewhere, we must submit to death in order to pass into fullness of life. Death is our great enemy, of course, but it is our last enemy. It separates us from all that we love—our bodies, our friends, our homeland, our family, our work, our play, our pleasures, our accomplishments, our desires, our laughter and sunshine, and everything else that we cling to that is good. We lose them all.

Lewis believed that everything really good that we have to let go of in death will be restored to us and amplified in our new, fuller life in heaven. It is as if the good things of life we love here are only a picture menu; after we lose the menu in death, we will be given the feast itself. And we can't quite imagine the real thing.

Some people fear that we won't be ourselves any longer in heaven.

But Lewis teaches that we will be more ourselves than ever there. Our *real* selves. Without pain and death and sorrow, of course, and also without any irritation or boredom. This life is a long dying, a frequent thirst. Once the dryness and dying are over, we will be forever flooded with the water of life.

Background of *The Last Battle*

C.S. Lewis wrote *The Last Battle* in 1953 and considered calling it *The Last King of Narnia*. His second choice was *Night Falls on Narnia*. His third proposal was *The Last Chronicle of Narnia*. Once again Lewis's titles with the word Narnia in them were rejected by his publisher. This time Lewis found his title by quoting a phrase from the book. Lewis no doubt realized that the words *The Last Battle* have more than one potential meaning for readers who think about it.

Ten years after he wrote this book, Lewis was in very bad health. He answered a letter from an American child named Ruth Broady who was hoping for more stories of Narnia.

> I'm so thankful that you realized the 'hidden story' in the Narnian books. It is odd, children nearly always do, grownups hardly ever. I'm afraid the Narnian series has come to an end, and am sorry to tell you that you can expect no more. God bless you.

Twenty-seven days later, C.S. Lewis died.

Key Symbol: the Stable

Key symbols in the stories so far have been the Fruit of the Tree of Life, the Stone Table, Living Water, the Door in the Air, the Spell in the Magic Book and a Shield of Faith. Some of these symbols are present again in *The Last Battle*, but a new one with special meaning is the Stable. ("Stable" is like an abbreviation of "Stone Table.") In contrast to Cair Paravel, the Stable is a small, dark, humble place. It is where Jesus entered mortal (animal) life. And it can symbolize the small dark place where we leave mortal (animal) life. It is human birth and death or death and birth.

In this story the Stable is used by evil powers in fraudulent and sinister ways, as a weapon, but ultimately the Stable is filled with the glory of God just as our death can be birth into far fuller life. In the Stable all find what they truly seek. Its inside is bigger than its outside. This is also true of human birth and death, humble and humbling as they are. This is a great mystery, a great comfort, and a great adventure.

The Last Battle and the Bible

What then shall we say to this? If God is for us, who is against us? He who did not spare his own Son but gave him up for us all, will he not also give us all things with him? Who shall bring any charge against God's elect? It is God who justifies; who is to condemn? Is it Christ Jesus, who died, yes, who was raised from the dead, who is at the right hand of God, who indeed intercedes for us? Who shall separate us from the love of Christ? Shall tribulation, or distress, or persecution, or famine, or nakedness, or peril, or sword? As it is written, "For thy sake we are being killed all the day long; we are regarded as sheep to be slaughtered."

No, in all these things we are more than conquerors through him who loved us. For I am sure that neither death, nor life, nor angels, nor principalities, nor things present, nor things to come, nor powers, nor height, nor depth, nor anything else in all creation, will be able to separate us from the love of God in Christ Jesus our Lord (Rom 8:31–39 RSV).

Lo! I tell you a mystery. We shall not all sleep, but we shall all be changed, in a moment, in the twinkling of an eye, at the last trumpet. For the trumpet will sound, and the dead

will be raised imperishable, and we shall be changed. For this
perishable nature must put on the imperishable, and this
mortal nature must put on immortality. When the perishable puts on the imperishable, and the mortal puts on
immortality, then shall come to pass the saying that is written: "Death is swallowed up in victory. O death, where is thy
victory? O death, where is thy sting?" The sting of death is
sin, and the power of sin is the law. But thanks be to God,
who gives us the victory through our Lord Jesus Christ
(1 Cor 15:51–57 RSV).

And I saw in the right hand of him who was seated on
the throne a scroll written within and on the back, sealed
with seven seals; and I saw a strong angel proclaiming with
a loud voice, "Who is worthy to open the scroll and break
its seals?" And no one in heaven or on earth or under the
earth was able to open the scroll or to look into it. Then one
of the elders said to me, "Weep not; lo, the Lion of the tribe
of Judah, the Root of David, has conquered, so that he can
open the scroll and its seven seals."

And between the throne and the four living creatures and
among the elders, I saw a Lamb standing, as though it had
been slain, with seven horns and with seven eyes, which are
the seven spirits of God sent out into all the earth; and he
went and took the scroll from the right hand of him who
was seated on the throne. And when he had taken the scroll,
the four living creatures and the twenty-four elders fell down
before the Lamb, each holding a harp, and with golden bowls
full of incense, which are the prayers of the saints; and they
sang a new song, saying, "Worthy art thou to take the scroll
and to open its seals, for thou wast slain and by thy blood
didst ransom men for God from every tribe and tongue and
people and nation, and hast made them a kingdom and
priests to our God, and they shall reign on earth."

Then I looked, and I heard around the throne and the living creatures and the elders the voice of many angels, numbering myriads of myriads and thousands of thousands, saying with a loud voice, "Worthy is the Lamb who was slain, to receive power and wealth and wisdom and might and honor and glory and blessing!" And I heard every creature in heaven and on earth and under the earth and in the sea, and all therein, saying, "To him who sits upon the throne and to the Lamb be blessing and honor and glory and might forever and ever!" And the four living creatures said, "Amen!" and the elders fell down and worshiped (Rev 5:1–14 RSV).

Special Vocabulary in *The Last Battle*

bath chair: wheelchair
blooming plant: polite slang for bloody deception
got the wind up: slang from 1915 meaning to become frightened
Guide: British Girl Scout
hack at rugger: kick at the shins in Rugby football
malapert: overly bold or saucy
mattocks: earth-breaking tools
moke: British slang for a donkey
panniers: pair of baskets
rive: split
rucked: wrinkled
slyboots: slang for a crafty person
'Ware danger: beware of danger
windscreen: windshield

A Favorite Quotation in *The Last Battle*

Lord Digory assured Lucy that all of the old Narnia that mattered had been drawn into the real Narnia through the Stable Door: "Of course it is different; as different as a real thing is from a shadow or as waking life is from a dream." Aslan's announced the glorious truth:

"The dream is ended; this is the morning."

As Aslan spoke, he no longer looked like a lion; and what began to happen then was beyond Lewis's power to describe. So these are the crowning words of the seven stories and what all good stories point toward.

Favorite Food in *The Last Battle*

There is probably no recipe left anywhere for stew made from wood pigeons and Wild Fresney weeds. In contrast, a wicked Ape's diet of oranges, bananas and nuts provides easy snacks. Readers could nibble daintily on mouse-size portions of cheese and wine and buttered oatmeal bread, such as Tirian received when he was bound to an ash tree. But the heartiest and simplest snack to accompany *The Last Battle* would be ordinary devilled-egg sandwiches and cheese sandwiches and meat-spread sandwiches such as those that were made in England and eaten in Narnia in this story. That was the ultimate takeout food.

Where and When in *The Last Battle*

Find Caldron Pool and the River of Narnia on your map. Do you know the way to the West?

The dates and numbers in the Narnian Chronicles don't fit together quite right. Tirian is not seventh in descent from Rilian, as he claims, if Rilian was Tirian's great-grandfather's great-grandfather, as Tirian also claims. It is rather like the math that Polly and Digory did which accidentally brought them to the wrong door and into Uncle Andrew's clutches. Someone is making little errors somewhere, and it could be Lewis himself. He utterly failed the math section on the entrance exam for Oxford and later got in anyway because he was a war veteran and brilliant in everything but math. (Ironically his mother had been a gifted mathematician.)

Peter and Edmund went to London to dig up the magic rings 49 years after Polly and Digory buried them. This story takes place in 1949 in England and 2555 in Narnia. It is about 200 years since Prince Rilian was rescued and became king, thanks to Eustace and Jill. They were both nine when they rescued Rilian, and now they are 16. Tirian is Rilian's great-great-great-great-grandson and is about 24 years old. At the time of this story Digory is 61, Polly is 60, Peter is 22, Edmund is 19 and Lucy is 17.

Do you believe that our human generation gaps will eventually be closed and we will be together at the prime of life permanently?

Four Main Parts of *The Last Battle*

1. Trouble in Narnia, chapters 1–4: three weeks
2. Hope from Our World, chapters 5–8: less than 48 hours
3. Utter Hopelessness on Stable Hill, chapters 9–12: one night
4. Farther Up and Farther In, chapters 13–15: timelessness

Facts and Ideas Concerning *The Last Battle*

1. *The Gift of Water*

This story is full of water. First was the Great Waterfall and Caldron Pool where the skin was found. Then Jewel likened a bad Aslan to "dry water." Mice dabbed their suffering king's face with water. The two children and Tirian found a fountain for drink and refreshment. Later they all suffered dreadful thirst hiding on Stable Hill and fighting the battle. At last they found a trickle and little pool at the white rock and while they were drinking (although doomed) they were perfectly happy and could not think of anything else. After the end of Narnia they found Emeth by a clear stream. Then they all plunged into the real Caldron Pool and swam up the Great Waterfall where thousands of tons of water poured down every second, diamonds and dark glassy green. And finally they saw that Aslan's country had green mountains and flashing waterfalls going up forever. And then Aslan himself came bounding down to them like a living water-fall of power and beauty to tell them that they could stay forever.

2. Scripture Pictures

The white rock, the great darkening of the sky, and Peter locking the door of heaven are all Bible images.

"To him who conquers . . . I will give him a white stone" (Rev 21:7 RSV). "Immediately after the tribulation of those days the sun will be darkened, and the moon will not give its light, and the stars will fall from heaven, and the powers of the heavens will be shaken; then will appear the sign of the Son of man in heaven, and then all the tribes of the earth will mourn, and they will see the Son of man coming on the clouds of heaven with power and great glory; and he will send out his angels with a loud trumpet call, and they will gather his elect from the four winds, from one end of heaven to the other" (Mt 24:29–31 RSV).

"And I tell you, you are Peter, and on this rock I will build my church, and the powers of death shall not prevail against it. I will give you the keys of the kingdom of heaven" (Mt 16:18–19 RSV).

3. Foolish Disguise

The idea of a donkey in a lion's skin is from an ancient fable. The Roman author Avianus used this plot in verse circa 400 A.D.

4. What's in a Name?

"Emeth" is the Hebrew word for truth. Emeth was a person with a truthful heart, a truth-seeker. Is a truth-cherishing heart essential-ly the same thing as a pure heart? In a footnote in Appendix Two of this book, "Narnia: The Domain of C.S. Lewis's Beliefs," Canadian professor M.A. Manzalaoui explains why he suspects that Lewis's portrayal of Emeth was a Narnian transformation of himself.

5. The Paws That Refresh

"Courage, child: we are all between the paws of the true Aslan." Tir-ian said this to Jill when things were very bad. It is reminiscent of Rilian's words to Jill and Eustace in *The Silver Chair*, "Courage, friends. Whether we live or die Aslan will be our good lord." The image of resting between the paws of Aslan gives some readers courage in hard times.

6. *Poetry*

The last two lines of a Narnian marching song are quoted in *The Last Battle*. Lewis evidently wrote "March for Drum, Trumpet, and Twenty-one Giants" in 1953 when he wrote *The Last Battle*; and he published it in the November 4, 1953 issue of *Punch* magazine. This poem can also be read in Lewis's book *Poems*; there the thumping march for giants is preceded by a delightful trotting march for dwarfs. But the book was published after Lewis's death, and there are unfortunate changes in many of Lewis's poems. The 1953 version of the giants' march is definitely better than the clumsy revision.

C.S. Lewis said he considered Robert Frost one of the very best contemporary poets. It seems probable that he was impressed by Robert Frost's nine-line poem "Fire and Ice," about the destruction of the world. Frost agrees with those who think the world will probably end in fire, because of the power of desire. But hate is great, and if the world had to perish twice, ice would suffice.

7. *End of History*

Author John Warwick Montgomery brought out a book in 1973 called *Where Is History Going? Essays in Support of the Historical Truths of Christian Revelation*. His dedication was "To the memory of C.S. Lewis, who Rightly Believed that the Fulfillment of History Takes Place in the Land of Narnia." In what sense is that dedication true?

8. *End of Time*

When gigantic Father Time arose from his dreams and blotted out the stars and sun, he had a new name. Many readers assume that his new name was Eternity.

9. *A Bad Influence?*

Some people have criticized the Narnian Chronicles for being unfair to dark people and females and for glorifying violence. What examples from the Chronicles inspired these three complaints? What facts about Lewis and his times exonerate Lewis? What would Lewis's response be if he heard these complaints today?

10. *A Bad Power*

Lewis believed in evil supernatural powers, in an actual devil. He believed that in some sense there is a real supernatural Tash moving in our world, as well as simple scoundrels like Shift. He also took the Bible seriously in its warning about a deceptive antichrist like "Tashlan." (Mt 24:23–27 warns against the false idea that Christ might return to earth privately somewhere.)

11. *Beyond Rules, Beyond Words*

"We've got to the country where everything is allowed." Lewis believed that in heaven we'll never have any wrong desires, that worship will be our central desire, and that worship will be joyful and exciting beyond words.

Factual Quiz Just for Fun

1. Jewel, King Tirian's best friend, was (a) a grey unicorn with a gold horn, (b) a great golden-bearded centaur, (c) a white unicorn with a blue horn.

2. When Tirian called for children to help him (a) Edmund and Lucy came through the wardrobe, (b) Jill and Eustace came without rings, (c) Polly and Digory came with rings.

3. The Ape was a traitor in league with (a) Calormen, (b) Archenland, (c) Lantern Waste.

4. Farsight the Eagle brought word that (a) Roonwit was killed and Cair Paravel captured, (b) Tash had come to Narnia, (c) Ginger was a traitor.

5. Rishda Tarkaan learned to his surprise and fear that the stable contained (a) a donkey, (b) Aslan, (c) Tash.

6. The dwarfs were for (a) Tirian, (b) the dwarfs, (c) Tash.

7. The seven English kings and queens of Narnia did *not* include (a) Polly Plummer, (b) Susan Pevensie, (c) Jill Pole.

8. Emeth, always seeking Tash, really belonged to (a) Aslan, (b) Calormen, (c) Tash.

9. Narnia finally died forever in (a) fire, (b) ice, (c) explosion.

10. The slogan of the new Narnia and the real England was (a) Hail Narnia! (b) aii-aii-aouwee! (c) farther up and farther in!

ANSWERS: 1 – c, 2 – b, 3 – a, 4 – a, 5 – c, 6 – b, 7 – b, 8 – a, 9 – b, 10 – c.

Thinking about Feelings

1. Tirian's password was: "The light is dawning, the lie broken." But it seemed that darkness and lies increased. How did you feel as things went from bad to worse in Narnia? (There have been readers who didn't have the heart to finish the book.) How appropriate is Tirian's password for today?

2. There are always people who say like Puzzle, "I only did what I was told." Some people like to obey orders and conform, and others don't. Which way is usually safer and more comfortable? Is this a matter of temperament, a matter of moral choice, or both?

3. Jewel the Unicorn said near his end, "If Aslan gave me my choice I would choose no other life than the life I have had and no other death than the one we go to." Can a person really be satisfied even in sorrow?

4. Roonwit's dying words were "remember that all worlds draw to an end and that noble death is a treasure which no one is too poor to buy." Is this traditional teaching still valid? Can there be nobility in death by slow illnesses?

5. When the children were temporarily feeling more cheerful, Lewis explained "one always feels better when one has made up one's

mind." He was unfamiliar with the Myers-Briggs temperament analysis which reveals that some people feel more comfortable before they make a decision and other people feel more comfortable afterwards. It is obvious which type Lewis was. This contrast causes some people to try to expedite decisions and causes others to delay them, which can obviously add stress to partnerships.

6. Many readers of *The Last Battle* are deeply disappointed by Susan's defection. A concerned nun wrote an eighth chronicle of Narnia called *The Centaur's Cavern*, telling about Susan's final trip to Narnia and how she became a heroic person. Some authorities objected, claiming that Lewis left no hope for Susan. They didn't realize that on January 22, 1957, Lewis wrote to an American boy named Martin that "there is plenty of time for Susan to mend, and perhaps she will get to Aslan's country in the end—in her own way."

7. On November 21, 1963, the day before he died, C.S. Lewis answered a letter from a boy named Philip. He said he was pleased that Philip and his parents liked his books. He added that children who wrote to him saw at once who Aslan was, but adults didn't.

The Last Battle As Inspiration

An American Boy

In 1955, before *The Last Battle* was published, an American child named Laurence Krieg became worried about the idea that he might be an idol-worshiper if he felt more love for Aslan than for Jesus. His mother wrote to Lewis for advice, and he sent her a long answer which is in the Wade Center at Wheaton College in Illinois. Lewis said that God knows quite well how hard we find it to love him more than anyone or anything else, and he won't be angry with us as long as we are trying. In fact he will help us.

But when Laurence thinks he is loving Aslan, he is really loving Jesus "and perhaps loving him more than he ever did before." The things he loves in Aslan, Lewis assures him, are really things in Jesus. And Laurence needn't worry if he likes a lion-body better than a man-body; that is natural for children and will pass with time. (Lewis mentions that if there are other worlds that need to be saved, Christ might indeed take other bodies we don't know about to save them.)

Lewis advised Laurence to pray that if his thoughts and feelings about the Narnian Chronicles were in some way bad, God would change them; but to pray for freedom from worry if nothing was wrong. Furthermore, he advised Laurence to pray for the kind of love that counts more than feelings—love that consists of doing what God wants and growing more Christ-like.

Lewis promised to pray for Laurence daily, and he said it would be kind and Christian-like if Laurence would pray, "if Mr. Lewis has worried any other children by his books or done them any harm, then please forgive him and help him never to do it again."

Remembering Lewis

In 1969 the Mythopoeic Society, an international organization based in Los Angeles, held a Narnian conference and picnic on what would have been C.S. Lewis's 71st birthday, six years after his death. Papers about Narnia were presented by people varying from a very young teenager to a middle-aged college professor. Nine of the essays were later printed in a booklet with Tim Kirk's handsome head of Aslan on the cover. Topics include Arthurian themes in the Narnian books, sin and hell in the Narnian books, the myth of Lilith in Narnia, the meaning of animals in Narnia, Narnia and Middle Earth, Narnia and Oz, and others.

A Person God Could Use

Ten years after Lewis's death, in 1973, a hundred people gathered in Santa Ana, California for a special meeting in memory of his ministry. At the end of their program of art, operatic-quality Narnian music and personal testimonies, they closed with the following tribute:

> C.S. Lewis was over 30 when he became a Christian. He never went to Bible school or seminary. He was never an

ordained minister or a trained theologian. He said he lacked the gift of evangelism. He worked full time in his secular profession and died before retirement age. Yet he ministers to us.

Since he left us we get new books about him and his writings every year. Courses on Lewis are offered in both Protestant and Catholic colleges. C.S. Lewis Societies, both formal and informal, have sprung up across the United States. People are reading his most recently published book and his first Christian book (*The Pilgrim's Regress*, 1933) and the 50 or so that came between. His sales are soaring.

But to Lewis it wasn't sales that counted; it was helping people. It wasn't records to set; it was truth to share. The goal wasn't fame; it was Joy. People, truth and Joy—that's C.S. Lewis all over. And if his view of the afterlife was correct, he is right now experiencing those three in ever new, ever more wonderful ways.

Benediction Based upon *The Last Battle*

Help us to be wiser than Puzzle and more prudent than Tirian;
But help us to be as humble as Puzzle and as noble as Tirian.
Preserve us from false doctrine and the antichrist.
Give us the courage to stand for the right against all odds.
Thank you that although all worlds end,
    no good thing is destroyed.
We are eager for the beginning of the real story.

PART THREE

APPENDICES

THE AUNT AND AMABEL

Preface by Kathryn Lindskoog

"The Aunt and Amabel" by Edith Nesbit was first published in *Blackie's Christmas Annual* late in 1908. C.S. Lewis probably read it there when he had just turned ten. He had already read many magical Nesbit stories and serials that appeared in *Strand Magazine*. In 1952, as Lewis was completing his Narnian chronicles, he said in a lecture, "When I was ten, I read fairy tales in secret and would have been ashamed if I had been found doing so. Now that I am 50 I read them openly." (It was up to his listeners to fill in the natural rejoinder if they were so inclined: "And now you write them openly, as well.")

Lewis never outgrew his early love for Edith Nesbit stories. On January 29, 1923, he wrote in his diary, "I dreamed that in a station waiting room I found a children's story by E. Nesbit; and became so interested that I missed my train." In his late 20s Lewis belatedly discovered her 1899 book *The Story of the Treasure Seekers* and its two sequels. He claimed to enjoy them then as much as he would have when he was a child. In the summer of 1948 Lewis remarked to his American friend Chad Walsh that he was writing a children's book "in the tradition of E. Nesbit." That was, of course, *The Lion, the Witch and the Wardrobe.*

Roger Lancelyn Green, Lewis's friend and biographer, read each of the Narnian books before it was published and offered many helpful observations. It was Green who named the series the Chronicles of Narnia and it was Green who reminded Lewis of "The Aunt and Amabel," which he had not consciously recalled when he wrote *The Lion, the Witch and the Wardrobe*. Buried in Lewis's memory for 40 years was the aunt's magic wardrobe that served as a station between worlds.

Near the end of *The Magician's Nephew* Aslan told Digory to pluck a magic Apple with healing power. Digory hurried back to his dying mother in London and fed it to her, then buried the core that evening in the back garden and marked the place. The next day he took Polly to see the place. "But, as it turned out, Digory need not have marked the place. Something was already coming up."

"The tree which sprang from the Apple that Digory had planted in the back garden, lived and grew into a fine tree." There was magic in its wood. "For when Digory was quite middle aged . . . there was a great storm all over the south of England which blew the tree down. He couldn't bear to have it simply chopped up into firewood, so he had part of the timber made into a wardrobe, which he put in his big house in the country. And though he himself did not discover the magic properties of the wardrobe, someone else did. That was the beginning of all the comings and goings between Narnia and our world, which you can read of in other books."

When Lewis read "The Aunt and Amabel" as a boy, he did not "mark the place" in his mind. But he didn't need to. "Something was already coming up." And when he was quite middle aged, he made part of the story into his own magic wardrobe, which he put in his big house in the country; and that was the beginning of all the comings and going between Narnia and our world for millions of readers to this day.

THE AUNT AND AMABEL

By Edith Nesbit

It is not pleasant to be a fish out of water. To be a cat in water is not what anyone would desire. To be in a temper is uncomfortable. And no one can fully taste the joys of life if he is in a Little Lord Fauntleroy suit. But by far the most uncomfortable thing to be in is disgrace, sometimes amusingly called Coventry by the people who are not in it.

We have all been there. It is a place where the heart sinks and aches, where familiar faces are clouded and changed, where any remark that one may tremblingly make is received with stony silence or with the assurance that nobody wants to talk to such a naughty child. If you are only in disgrace, and not in solitary confinement, you will creep about a house that is like the one you have had such jolly times in, and yet as unlike it as a bad dream is to a June morning. You will long to speak to people, and be afraid to speak. You will wonder whether there is anything you can do that will change things at all. You have said you are sorry, and that has changed nothing. You will wonder whether you are to stay forever in this desolate place, outside all hope and love and fun and happiness. And though it has happened before, and has always in the end come to an end, you can never be quite sure that this time it is not going to last forever.

"It *is* going to last forever," said Amabel, who was eight. "What shall I do? Oh whatever shall I do?"

What she *had* done ought to have formed the subject of her meditations. She had done what had seemed to her all the time, and in fact still seemed, a self-sacrificing and noble act. She was staying with an aunt—measles or a new baby or the painters in the house, I forget which, the cause of her banishment. And the aunt, who was really a great-aunt and quite old enough to know better, had been grumbling about her head gardener to a lady who called in blue spectacles and a beady bonnet with violet flowers in it.

"He hardly lets me have a plant for the table," said the aunt, "and that border in front of the breakfast-room window—it's just bare earth—and I expressly ordered chrysanthemums to be planted there. He thinks of nothing but his greenhouse."

The beady-violet-blue-glassed lady snorted, and said she didn't know what we were coming to and she would have just half a cup, please, with not quite so much milk, thank you very much.

Now what would you have done? Minded your own business most likely, and not got into trouble at all. Not so Amabel. Enthusiastically anxious to do something which should make the great-aunt see what a thoughtful, unselfish little girl she really was (the aunt's opinion of her being at present quite otherwise), she got up very early in the morning and took the cutting-out scissors from the workroom table drawer and stole, "like an errand of mercy," she told herself, to the greenhouse where she busily snipped off every single flower she could find. MacFarlane was at his breakfast. Then with the points of the cutting-out scissors she made nice deep little holes in the flower bed where the chrysanthemums ought to have been, and stuck the flowers in—chrysanthemums, geraniums, primulas, orchids, and carnations. It would be a lovely surprise for Auntie.

Then the aunt came down to breakfast and saw the lovely surprise. Amabel's world turned upside down and inside out suddenly and surprisingly and there she was, in Coventry, and not even the housemaid would speak to her. Her great-uncle, whom she passed in the hall on her way to her own room, did indeed, as he smoothed his hat, murmur, "Sent to Coventry, eh? Never mind, it'll soon be over," and went off to the City banging the front door behind him.

He meant well, but he did not understand.

Amabel understood, or she thought she did, and knew in her miserable heart that she was sent to Coventry for the last time, and that this time she would stay there.

"I don't care," she said quite untruly. "I'll never try to be kind to any one again." And that wasn't true either. She was to spend the whole day alone in the best bedroom, the one with the four-post bed and the red curtains and the large wardrobe with a looking glass in it that you could see yourself in to the very ends of your strap-shoes.

The first thing Amabel did was to look at herself in the glass. She was still sniffing and sobbing and her eyes were swimming in tears. Another one rolled down her nose as she looked—that was very interesting. Another rolled down and that was the last, because as soon as you get interested in watching your tears they stop.

Next she looked out of the window and saw the decorated flower bed, just as she had left it, very bright and beautiful.

"Well, it *does* look nice," she said. "I don't care what they say."

Then she looked round the room for something to read; there was nothing. The old-fashioned best bedrooms never did have anything. Only on the large dressing table, on the left-hand side of the oval swing-glass, was one book covered in red velvet and on it very twistily embroidered in yellow silk and mixed up with misleading leaves and squiggles were the letters, A.B.C.

"Perhaps it's a picture alphabet," said Amabel, quite pleased, though of course she was much too old to care for alphabets. Only when one is very unhappy and very dull, anything is better than nothing. She opened the book.

"Why, it's only a [train] time-table!" she said. "I suppose it's for people when they want to go away and Auntie puts it here in case they suddenly make up their minds to go and feel that they can't wait another minute. I feel like that, only it's no good, and I expect other people do too."

She had learned how to use the dictionary and this seemed to go the same way. She looked up the names of all the places she knew— Brighton where she had once spent a month, Rugby where her brother was at school and Home, which was Amberley—and she saw the times when the trains left for these places and wished she could go by those trains.

And once more she looked round the best bedroom which was her prison and thought of the Bastille and wished she had a toad to tame, like the poor Viscount, or a flower to watch growing, like Picciola.

She was very sorry for herself and very angry with her aunt and very grieved at the conduct of her parents—she had expected better things from them—and now they had left her in this dreadful place where no one loved her and no one understood her.

There seemed to be no place for toads or flowers in the best room, it was carpeted all over even in its least noticeable corners. It had everything a best room ought to have—and everything was of dark shining mahogany. The toilet-table had a set of red and gold glass things— a tray, candlesticks, a ring-stand, many little pots with lids, and two bottles with stoppers. When the stoppers were taken out they smelt very strange, something like very old scent, and something like cold cream also very old, and something like going to the dentist's.

I do not know whether the scent of those bottles had anything to do with what happened. It certainly was a very extraordinary scent. Quite different from any perfume that I smell nowadays, but I remember that when I was a little girl I smelt it quite often. But then there are no best rooms now such as there used to be. The best rooms now are gay with chintz and mirrors, and there are always flowers and books, and little tables to put your teacup on and sofas and armchairs. And they smell of varnish and new furniture.

When Amabel had sniffed at both bottles and looked in all the pots, which were quite clean and empty except for a pearl button and two pins in one of them, she took up the A.B.C. again to look for Whitby where her godmother lived. And it was then that she saw the extraordinary name *"Whereveryouwantogoto."* This was odd—but the name of the station from which it started was still more extraordinary, for it was not Euston or Cannon Street or Marylebone.

The name of the station was *"Bigwardrobeinspareroom."* And below this name, really quite unusual for a station, Amabel read in small letters:

"Single fares strictly forbidden. Return tickets No Class Nuppence. Trains leave *Bigwardrobeinspareroom* all the time."

And under that in still smaller letters—*"You had better go now."*

What would you have done? Rubbed your eyes and thought you were dreaming? Well, if you had, nothing more would have happened.

Nothing ever does when you behave like that. Amabel was wiser. She went straight to the Big Wardrobe and turned its glass handle.

"I expect it's only shelves and people's best hats," she said. But she only said it. People often say what they don't mean, so that if things turn out as they don't expect, they can say "I told you so", but this is most dishonest to one's self, and being dishonest to one's self is almost worse than being dishonest to other people. Amabel would never have done it if she had been herself. But she was out of herself with anger and unhappiness.

Of course it wasn't hats. It was, most amazingly, a crystal cave, very oddly shaped like a railway station. It seemed to be lighted by stars, which is, of course, unusual in a booking office and over the station clock was a full moon. The clock had no figures, only *Now* in shining letters all round it, twelve times, and the *Nows* touched, so the clock was bound to be always right. How different from the clock you go to school by!

A porter in white satin hurried forward to take Amabel's luggage. Her luggage was the A.B.C. which she still held in her hand.

"Lots of time, Miss," he said, grinning in a most friendly way, "I *am* glad you're going. You *will* enjoy yourself! What a nice little girl you are!"

This was cheering. Amabel smiled.

At the pigeon-hole that tickets come out of, another person, also in white satin, was ready with a mother-of-pearl ticket, round, like a card counter.

"Here you are, Miss," he said with the kindest smile, "price nothing, and refreshments free all the way. It's a pleasure," he added, "to issue a ticket to a nice little lady like you." The train was entirely of crystal, too, and the cushions were of white satin. There were little buttons such as you have for electric bells, and on them *"Whatyou-wantoeat," "Whatyouwantodrink," "Whatyouwantoread,"* in silver letters.

Amabel pressed all the buttons at once, and instantly felt obliged to blink. The blink over, she saw on the cushion by her side a silver tray with vanilla ice, boiled chicken and white sauce, almonds (blanched), peppermint creams, and mashed potatoes, and a long glass of lemonade—beside the tray was a book. It was Mrs. Ewing's *Bad-tempered Family* and it was bound in white vellum.

There is nothing more luxurious than eating while you read— unless it be reading while you eat. Amabel did both: they are not the same thing, as you will see if you think the matter over.

And just as the last thrill of the last spoonful of ice died away, and the last full stop of the *Bad-tempered Family* met Amabel's eye, the train stopped, and hundreds of railway officials in white velvet shouted, *"Whereyouwantogoto!* Get out!"

A velvety porter, who was somehow like a silkworm as well as like a wedding handkerchief sachet, opened the door.

"Now!" he said, "come on out, Miss Amabel, unless you want to go to '*Whereyoudon'twantogoto.*'"

She hurried out on to an ivory platform.

"Not on the ivory, if you please," said the porter, "the white Ax-minster carpet—it's laid down expressly for you."

Amabel walked along it and saw ahead of her a crowd, all in white.

"What's all that?" she asked the friendly porter.

"It's the Mayor, dear Miss Amabel," he said. "with your address."

"My address is The Old Cottage, Amberley," she said, "at least it used to be"—and found herself face-to-face with the Mayor. He was very like Uncle George, but he bowed low to her, which was not Uncle George's habit, and said: "Welcome, dear little Amabel. Please accept this admiring address from the Mayor and burgesses and apprentices and all the rest of it, of *Whereyouwantogoto.*"

The address was in silver letters, on white silk, and it said: "Welcome, dear Amabel. We know you meant to please your aunt. It was very clever of you to think of putting the greenhouse flowers in the bare flower bed. You couldn't be expected to know that you ought to ask leave before you touch other people's things."

"Oh, but," said Amabel quite confused. "I did . . ."

But the band struck up and drowned her words. The instruments of the band were all of silver and the bandsmen's clothes of white leather. The tune they played was "Cheero!"

Then Amabel found that she was taking part in a procession, hand in hand with the Mayor and the band playing like mad all the time. The Mayor was dressed entirely in cloth of silver and as they went along he kept saying, close to her ear, "You have our sympathy, you have our sympathy" till she felt quite giddy.

There was a flower show—all the flowers were white. There was a concert—all the tunes were old ones. There was a play called *Put yourself in her place*. And there was a banquet with Amabel in the place of honor.

They drank her health in white wine whey and then through the Crystal Hall of a thousand gleaming pillars, where thousands of guests, all in white, were met to do honor to Amabel, the shout went up—"Speech, speech!"

I cannot explain to you what had been going on in Amabel's mind. Perhaps you know. Whatever it was it began like a very tiny butterfly in a box, that could not keep quiet, but fluttered, and fluttered, and fluttered. And when the Mayor rose and said: "Dear Amabel, you whom we all love and understand; dear Amabel, you who were so unjustly punished for trying to give pleasure to an unresponsive aunt; poor, ill-used, ill-treated, innocent Amabel; blameless, suffering Amabel, we await your words," that fluttering, tiresome butterfly-thing inside her seemed suddenly to swell to the size and strength of a fluttering albatross, and Amabel got up from her seat of honor on the throne of ivory and silver and pearl and said, choking a little, and extremely red about the ears—"Ladies and gentlemen, I don't want to make a speech, I just want to say, 'Thank you,' and to say—to say—to say . . ."

She stopped and all the white crowd cheered.

"To say," she went on as the cheers died down, "that I wasn't blameless, and innocent, and all those nice things. I ought to have thought. And they *were* Auntie's flowers. But I did want to please her. It's all so mixed. Oh, I wish Auntie was here!"

And instantly Auntie *was* there, very tall and quite nice-looking, in a white velvet dress and an ermine cloak.

"Speech," cried the crowd. "Speech from Auntie!"

Auntie stood on the step of the throne beside Amabel, and said: "I think, perhaps, I was hasty. And I think Amabel meant to please me. But all the flowers that were meant for the winter . . . well—I was annoyed. I'm sorry."

"Oh, Auntie, so am I—so am I," cried Amabel, and the two began to hug each other on the ivory step, while the crowd cheered like mad, and the band struck up that well-known air, "If you only understood!"

"Oh, Auntie," said Amabel among hugs, "This is such a lovely place, come and see everything. We may, mayn't we?" she asked the Mayor.

"The place is yours," he said, "and now you can see many things that you couldn't see before. We are The People who Understand. And now you are one of Us. And your aunt is another."

I must not tell you all that they saw because these things are secrets only known to The People who Understand and perhaps you do not yet belong to that happy nation. And if you do, you will know without my telling you.

And when it grew late, and the stars were drawn down, somehow, to hang among the trees, Amabel fell asleep in her aunt's arms beside a white foaming fountain on a marble terrace, where white peacocks came to drink.

*　*　*

She awoke on the big bed in the spare room, but her aunt's arms were still round her.

"Amabel," she was saying, "Amabel!"

"Oh, Auntie," said Amabel sleepily, "I am so sorry. It *was* stupid of me. And I did mean to please you."

"It *was* stupid of you," said the aunt, "but I am sure you meant to please me. Come down to supper." And Amabel has a confused recollection of her aunt's saying that she was sorry, adding, "Poor little Amabel."

If the aunt really did say it, it was fine of her. And Amabel is quite sure that she did say it.

✻   ✻   ✻

Amabel and her great-aunt are now the best of friends. But neither of them has ever spoken to the other of the beautiful city called *"Whereyouwantogoto."* Amabel is too shy to be the first to mention it, and no doubt the aunt has her own reasons for not broaching the subject.

But of course they both know that they have been there together, and it is easy to get on with people when you and they alike belong to the *Peoplewhounderstand.*

✻   ✻   ✻

If you look in the A.B.C. that your people have you will not find a *"Whereyouwantogoto."* It is only in the red velvet bound copy that Amabel found in her aunt's best bedroom.

NARNIA:
THE DOMAIN OF
LEWIS'S BELIEFS

By M.A. Manzalaoui

(Dr. Manzalaoui was an Oxford University pupil of C.S. Lewis immediately after World War II, from 1945 to 1948. Before his recent retirement he served as a professor of English at the University of British Columbia in Vancouver, British Columbia. This essay first appeared in a slightly different version in the spring 1995 issue of the *Canadian C.S. Lewis Journal*.)

* * *

Lewis's students were taken by surprise when he published *The Lion, The Witch and the Wardrobe* late in 1950 in time for the Christmas-present trade. Since the 20s, Lewis had published poetry, religious books and critical and historical works concerning English literature, including a ground-breaking work on medieval allegorical love literature. He had been an outstanding lecturer and tutor in English literature, in philosophy and political theory. But none of us associated this bachelor don with any interest in children.

The indications, however, were there for people to notice. He had already written science-fiction—another form of fantasy. He was known to be a friend and associate of J.R.R. Tolkien, who had published *The Hobbit* before the war. He was interested in nonrealistic fiction. Further reasons for turning to children's fantasies are given by Lewis himself in his critical essays: principally he writes with typical common-sense that sometimes "a children's story is the best art form for something you have to say."

Of this method he says that there came into his mind the picture of Mr. Tumnus in the woods, or rather of a faun—the classical deity with horns and tail—carrying parcels and an umbrella. Other pictures followed spontaneously. Then the pictures joined up to form a story—rather, I suppose, like pictures in a comic strip cartoon. But where gaps remained, his deliberate inventing had to come into play. The personality of the adult writer and of the child who is conceived of as the reader came together to create a composite personality which produced the book.

Of the content he writes that nonhuman characters present human "types" more succinctly than realistic ones, implying that nonrealism can, so to speak, be more successfully true to life than realism: "As for the genre of the fairy tale, it can add to one's perception of the actual world a new dimension, that of depth." Given all this, one cannot neglect in addition the considerable influence of Tolkien's essay "On Fairy-Stories," which we shall come to towards the end of this essay. Lewis insists on our not treating the story merely as surface, concealing and *meaning* something else. Further meaning than the immediate is there, but not to be dug out by a process that scratches out the surface meaning and forms an intellectual puzzle. In other words, we are not dealing with an allegory or an imitation of truth, but the creating of a secondary world which works upon us by our enjoying it for its own sake.

It might be thought that as a scholar of medieval allegory, Lewis set out to create continuous, consistent and strict allegory here, but he has not. (The term *"strict* allegory" I take from Dr. Richard Purtill of Western Washington University—I wish to acknowledge a debt to him which he would recognize here and elsewhere in this essay.)

I believe that there is occasional allegory here, and it occurs at important points in the narrative. The chief points are the following: First, in the concluding Narnian book, *The Last Battle*, the final and glorious apocalypse in which cosmic Narnia is destroyed and reborn as the supernal Narnia: a fairy-tale version of chapters 14–22 of the *Book of Revelation*. Second, at the climax of *The Lion, The Witch and the Wardrobe*, the Atonement for Edmund's treachery by Aslan, Aslan's Dejection, the Stations of his ordeal, his slaying, the visit of the women, or rather, the two girls, to his resting place and his Resurrection. This is so close to the biblical accounts that it is astonishing to learn from Lewis himself that there are readers who failed to see the connection with the Crucifixion and the Resurrection. I can testify as a fact that the wife of a university colleague of mine said to me that she couldn't recall anything particularly Christian about *The Lion, The Witch and the Wardrobe*.

It is true, nevertheless, that the general method of the *Chronicles of Narnia is* not allegory—not loose allegory, and emphatically not the strict allegory of the medievals and of Spenser, with its layers of fourfold meaning. Perhaps some term such as *transposition, similitude* or *counterpart* could be used for those elements in the *Narnia* stories which have a symbolic meaning—or one could use Dorothy L. Sayers's term *symbolic image*, which she uses for those of the features of Dante's *Divine Comedy* which are not allegorical. I stress this, because a search for allegorical meaning in every detail of Lewis's stories will lead one wildly astray—just as the attempt to impose strict and continuous allegory upon the New Testament parables breaks down—to accept that you would have to believe that Jesus Christ thought it sinful not to wear evening dress at a formal party, and thought it wrong not to invest one's friend's money in the stock market, a conclusion we will reach if we misread the Parable of the Wedding Feast and the Parable of the Talents. Another reason for stressing the point is to caution against a present-day tendency to employ the word *allegory* for every use of features in any way remotely symbolic, to look for a skeletal program behind a story or poem, and ignore the work of art itself, and the width of the range of different forms of symbolism.

Let us note in this connection that Lewis wrote: "Let pictures tell their own moral. It'll rise from spiritual roots you have succeeded in striking during the whole course of your life."

It is clear from Lewis's essay "On Writing for Children" that he set out on a double task: to treat child readers as the personalities and interests of children require, but never to patronize a child-reader, a particularly difficult task for a bachelor university teacher whose contact with children was not close. He jokes in the same essay about Arthur Mee, the editor of the *Children's Encyclopedia* and *Children's Newspaper,* under whose weight of writings I myself suffered for much of my boyhood, that he has "been told that Arthur Mee never met a child and never wished to." It seems to me that Lewis succeeds in his stories because he is speaking to the child that he remembers having been. This, by the way, is combined in *The Lion, The Witch, and the Wardrobe* with Lewis's also representing his own views, and those of his friend Charles Williams, in the character of the Professor—the grown-up who understands the veracity and the importance for the children of having had their everyday life traversed by an experience of the beyond. If you have only read *The Lion, the Witch and the Wardrobe,* which is the first of the *Narnia Chronicles,* it will not be clear to you that the story grows more profound as it develops, as a study of human spiritual growth, and of the position of humankind in relation to the universe and to God.

That is a grandiose claim to make for a series of seven children's stories. So it may be as well, before proceeding further, to mention some of the faults and limitations of the Narnia books. A North American reader in the 1990s will notice that the stories are firmly set in Britain during and immediately after the Second World War. The Pevensie children are staying at the Professor's (as children had stayed in Lewis's household) because of the arrangement made, just before the outbreak of war, to evacuate children from threatened cities to safe havens. The reader is expected to understand how small Lucy's handkerchief seems to Giant Rumblebuffin by being told it was only about the same size to him that a saccharine tablet would be to you— a familiarity brought about, not by attempts to slim, but by sugar rationing. This is not blameworthy, but the firmly genteel and upper-middle class perspective may be found irritating. In *Prince Caspian* we read, "Whatever hothouses *your people* may have, you have never tasted such grapes"; in *The Magician's Nephew* Lewis himself sounds like his airhead character Lasaraleen of *The Horse and His Boy* when he jauntily says, "Everyone had lots of servants in those days."

There are inconsistencies between one book and another as to who were the first earthlings to reach Narnia; an inconsistency can be found within a tale: the Witch is unfamiliar with the door to the world of humans at one point in *The Lion, The Witch and The Wardrobe*, five pages later she shows she is familiar with it. More seriously, am I alone among readers of *The Dawn Treader* in finding the treatment of the one-legged Dufflepuds rather callous, reduced as they are to hopping about on a single leg as a penalty for their stupidity, and for the amusement of others?

More seriously, in *The Horse and His Boy*, the pseudo-oriental nation of the Calormenes is shown as having an unpleasant religion, an invented one but one which in many ways is a parody of features taken from Hinduism, Islam and the religion of the ancient Canaanites, and they have a culture resembling the Indian and Middle Eastern cultures. Although the Calormenes are given some good qualities, they have unattractive traits based on the personal habits of less respectable Middle Easterners—for instance, they smell "of garlic and onions." Here I must plead a personal reaction, since this is a hostile Western view of my own cultural background. It is true, however, that this view is counterbalanced in *The Last Battle* by an important theological act of latitude which I wish to come back to. Notice, nevertheless the quite unfair stress on the *power* rather than the *mercy* of the Calormene god Tash. Lewis takes the Moslem invocation: "In the name of God, the *compassionate*, the *merciful*," and turns it into the Calormene formula, "In the name of Tash, the *irresistible*, the *inexorable*."

But it is time to turn to more positive points. Let us note now the basic governing pattern of every one of the Narnia stories—closeness of the supernatural, the divine, to the mundane, the everyday, the humdrum. The normal pattern in a Narnia story is for a number of children to be whisked out of their ordinary lives, to find themselves voluntarily taking part in a quest with a very serious and lofty purpose in which their spiritual growth is an outstanding factor. In some cases a child who is gravely guilty—such as Edmund in *The Lion, The Witch and the Wardrobe*—reforms and becomes heroic. The children meet Aslan at important junctures in the quest and have a closer encounter with him at the conclusion.

I cannot tell if the episodic meetings, the warnings and guidance of Aslan are meant to be a parallel to prevenient grace, while the climactic meetings are analogues to what is called "efficacious" grace, but the conclusion of *The Last Battle* certainly parallels the Beatific Vision granted to the redeemed. In terms of the art of story-telling, the narrative itself in the same way proceeds from level to level of dignity. Early in the story there is cozy homeliness the wardrobe in the Professor's house on earth, Mr. Tumnus's tea and sardines on toast, Mrs. Beaver with her sewing machine, her fried trout and boiled potatoes; in the middle of the book there is a deal of romantic questing. Edmund's entry into the Witch's House, the sight of the animals that have been turned to stone, the children's trek through the wilds as the age-old winter breaks resplendently into spring. Then comes the battle of Cair Paravel, and finally we move from the heroics of that fight to the spiritual battle of the submission, death and resurrection of Aslan.

In the same way, published a year before Lewis's first sketching of the plan of *The Lion, The Witch and the Wardrobe*, Tolkien's *The Hobbit* proceeds from the domestic to the romantic and on to the epic, from Hobbiton to the Misty Mountains and Mirkwood, on to the Battle of the Five Armies—though, in its case, there is no *openly* spiritual development. To keep the child reader anchored to everyday life, however high-flying the spiritual adventures become, there are the ordinary objects which play important roles in the stories—the wardrobe as the gateway to Narnia, the London street lamppost which is growing in the woods in Narnia.[1]

Domestic imagery is also involved in some of the similes and reflections; so in *The Silver Chair* we have helpful references to the sounds of a vacuum cleaner and of an old-fashioned radio as it warms up and to the feel of the second half of morning school, after break. Most striking, in returning us to the everyday, is the closing sentence of *Prince Caspian*, Edmund's remark when he finds himself back in an English railway station, "Bother! I've left my new torch in Narnia."

And, throughout, to produce comedy and poetry, there is the common technique of the use of fantasies by which the ordinary world and the secondary world are seen in double vision. So, in *The Silver Chair*, a younger owl says that he expects the wise old Glimfeather to say "You're a mere chick. I remember you when you were an egg. Don't come trying to teach *me*, Sir." And in *Prince Caspian* we learn that talking trees have a varied menu of soils and waters, "rich brown loam . . . like chocolate," at the cheese stage of a meal "a chalky soil," for a sweet "the finest gravels powdered with choice silver sand." And a centaur satisfies his human stomach with a meal like ours, and his second stomach, the horse one, with fresh grass. This is the pseudo-realism of fantasy, the realism of presentation, as distinct from the realism of content.

---

[1] My own notion is that the Narnian lamppost is derived from a Victorian gas lamppost which stands in a field in Newnham, Cambridge, between the river and the pathway to Grantchester. [This area is described on page 278 of the 1975 edition of *Illustrated Guide to Britain*, published by Drive Publications Limited for the Automobile Association. "Grantchester: A serene little village of thatch, timber and plaster, loved by so many generations of tutors and undergraduates that it has become almost an integral part of Cambridge. It can be reached by crossing the floodgate at the bottom of Mill Lane, branching from the towpath towards Newnham Road, through Grantchester Street and Grantchester Meadows and then by a footpath across the meadows. In the old vicarage the poet Rupert Brooke lived and wrote before the First World War. Just outside the village, on the Trumpington road, is a signpost pointing to Byron's Pool. The muddy cut, by which sat not only Byron but predecessors such as Chaucer, Spenser, Milton, and Dryden, is less attractive than the paths to it through the coppice, rustling with squirrels."] The field with the lamppost is surrounded by trees,

But unreal fantasies as the *Narnia Chronicles* are, they demonstrate a clear understanding of human psychology, as telling as the symbolic entities and the metaphysical truths. The children, heroic at their best, are often frightened and sometimes quarrel and are bad tempered. We recognize the joyless nonbeliever's puritanism in the Witch's complaint against partying: "What is the meaning of all this gluttony, this waste, this self-indulgence?" And we can all recognize our own responses in reflections like these:

> "Children have one kind of silliness . . . and grownups have another kind" or "One usually gets on better with people when one is making plans than when one is talking about nothing in particular" or (of seeing the wicked but mortal Uncle Andrew together with the diabolical witch Jadis) "One good thing about seeing the two together was that you would never again be afraid of Uncle Andrew, any more than you'd be afraid of a worm after you had met a rattlesnake or afraid of a cow after you had met a mad bull."

As a retired professor who is attempting to continue with academic productiveness, I found one remark most relevant of all—it's about emancipation from slavery:

> One of the worst results of being a slave and being forced to do things is that when there is no one to force you any

---

and gives the appearance of a clearing in the woods. What is a lamppost doing there? In some winters the River Cam overflows its banks and floods the bathing place and the field beyond it. If there is a frost, the floodwater freezes over, providing a very safe opportunity for skating (over a few inches of water only). Nighttime skating was a favorite Victorian sport, and, to make it possible, the municipality placed a lamppost in the middle of the field. I've not heard of the lamp being lit in our lifetime. [In winter C.S. Lewis sometimes went ice-skating on the pond in his own woods at The Kilns. These woods are commonly assumed to have served as inspiration for the woods in Narnia. Because the Newnham lamppost was once known to many academics, it is not unlikely that Lewis was aware of it; and if he was aware of it, he had no doubt visualized it. Therefore the lonely lamppost in a clearing in Narnia may have been inspired by the lonely lamppost in a clearing near Cambridge.]

more you find you have almost lost the power of forcing yourself.

In fact, Lewis is never far from his own everyday life in the Narnia books. The loyal but grumpy Puddleglum the Marshwiggle, a character in *The Silver Chair,* is based on his own gardener Paxford. But there is another source that provided a large number of details to the Narnia tales, and that is the canon of traditional literature which Lewis also lived in, as reader and as teacher. Some details are significant, others are marginal and playful, but all serve the important purpose of setting the *Chronicles* in a self-invigorating tradition of mainly European imaginative works.

In *The Voyage of the Dawn Treader* Aslan appears in the form of a lamb and provides fish broiling on a fire, "the most delicious food [the children] had ever tasted." In *The Lion, The Witch and the Wardrobe* Aslan provides the huge crowd of revivified statues with "a fine high tea at about eight o'clock." The gospel parallels are obvious there and important. But elsewhere, sometimes only in details of imagery, language or passing incident, I find the following mixed bag of sources: Homer, Plato, Virgil, *The Arabian Nights,* Beowulf, the Middle English romances of *Sir Orfeo, Sir Gawain* and *Havelock,* Malory's *Morte d'Arthur,* at least three of Chaucer's poems, Dante, Shakespeare, Milton, Wagner, *Alice in Wonderland, Huckleberry Finn,* Richmond Crompton's William (and if a North American audience do not recognize that reference, I can feel only pity for them), and Lewis's own friends Charles Williams and Tolkien.

There is one model which is more integral to the pattern of the Narnia stories and to their theology—Edmund Spenser's *Faërie Queene.* In each of the six completed books of this romance epic, a hero undertakes a chivalric quest for the good of others and growing in heroic and in spiritual stature he achieves a great deal through his own effort. But at the true crisis of the tale, faced with the full power of evil, the hero cannot succeed on his own. To complete the quest, Prince Arthur intervenes, rescues the hero and causes his efforts to come to a happy conclusion. For the purposes of this function,

Arthur can be recognized as the allegorical figure of faith, of grace or of the Redeemer, taking over where human will and initiative are beyond being of any avail.

Similarly in the *Narnia Chronicles*, the hero's growth, their initiative, are essential to the solution and they are left to their own devices by Aslan until the moment which he was waiting for, when he intervenes: good works, and then grace. Notice, by the way, that in Tolkien's *The Lord of the Rings*, never far from Lewis's mind, Frodo who has heroically set out to destroy the One Ring, when he eventually, after countless achievements, reaches the Cracks of Doom, doesn't throw the ring down. He is tempted to keep it and put its power to selfish use. It is Gollum's attempt to seize it—Gollum unknowingly being used by a power never mentioned by Tolkien—which sends it down the Cracks, to its destruction.

With this point, we are at the heart of the theology of the Narnia books. Human beings, forced by their good natures into vocations they never expected to adopt, conquer fear, persevere, grow in ability, determination and courage, but they often fail—yet there is virtue in such failure for it brings about the intervention of grace. Aslan, as Lewis says, comes bounding in. In fact, the virtuous actions were all along really the actions of Aslan; as Mr. Beaver says to the children, "It is he, not you, that will save Mr. Tumnus."

Fortune is all providence: the Hermit in *The Horse and His Boy* says, "Daughter . . . I have now lived a hundred and nine winters in this world and have never yet met any such thing as Luck." The development of the child heroes is, of course, not as straightforward as a rapid summary suggests. Edmund is greedy and a traitor, jealous of his elder brother, eager for kingship and Turkish delight, but an early sign of his conversion comes when he sees the creatures that have been turned to stone and "for the first time in this story" feels "sorry for someone besides himself." In a later story, Eustace goes through a similar conversion.

The characters who are predominantly good undergo temptation, and are blameworthy: Peter excuses Edmund to Aslan when he confesses that it was because he, Peter, had shown Edmund that he was angry with him, that he "helped him go wrong"—Peter's recognition of his own wrong action in its turn helps Peter towards self-purifying. In *The Voyage of the Dawn Treader*, Caspian and Edmund are tempted by the black magic of Deathwater Island and fall into a quarrel which stops when Aslan glides across the hillside above them. In the Edwardian flashback which is *The Magician's Nephew*, the boy Digory Kirke, whom we know in the 1940s in *The Lion, The Witch, and the Wardrobe* as the aged Professor, restrains himself from eating the apple of life and takes it back to earth to save his mother's life and to plant the seeds of the tree from which the Wardrobe is going to be made. In *The Horse and His Boy* Aravis cannot escape receiving scratches from the Lion's own claws on her back, "equal to the stripes" received by "her stepmother's slave because of the drugged sleep Aravis cast upon her as part of her successful plan to escape from Calormen." Sadly, Susan falls away altogether into grown-up vanity and is not granted the happiness that follows for the others after they are killed in a railway crash. (Though one can hope that in years to come she will be re-converted.)

It is fitting in children's literature with metaphysical implications that the sins of the main characters should be this blend of outwardly slight peccadillos and deeper sins. The same blend is found in the Narnian equivalent of human intimacy with God. Lucy and Susan romp with Aslan and snuggle into his mane and have him tossing them into the air and catching them in his paws, but "whether it was more like playing with a thunderstorm or playing with a kitten Lucy could never make up her mind." A mixture of the awesome and the joyful is the constant characteristic of the Aslan-experience, the Narnian form of that inward act of enlightenment which is a recurrent theme in Lewis's writings and which he calls "numinous awe": the loving and joyful fear of the protective power of God. Mr. and Mrs. Beaver try to explain the paradox to the Pevensie children:

> [Susan] "Is he quite safe? I shall feel rather nervous about meeting a lion." "That you will, dearie, and no mistake," said

Mrs. Beaver; "if there's anyone who can appear before Aslan without their knees knocking, they're either braver than most or else just silly." "Then he isn't safe?" said Lucy. "Safe?" said Mr. Beaver; "don't you hear what Mrs. Beaver tells you? Who said anything about safe? "Course he isn't safe. But he's good. He's the king, I tell you." "I'm longing to see him," said Peter, "even if I do feel frightened when it comes to the point."

Lewis had read Kenneth Grahame's *Wind in the Willows* as an adult and he must have recognized in it his own feeling which he describes in his autobiography when he read of Ratty and Mole's encounter with the god Pan as he plays his pipes over the strayed and sleeping otter child. In the Narnia books no passage is more famous that the one in *The Silver Chair* in which Jill meets Aslan for the first time. Very thirsty, she has come to a stream, but finds a talking Lion lying in her way:

> And the thirst became so bad that she almost felt she would not mind being eaten by the Lion if only she could be sure of getting a mouthful of water first. "If you're thirsty, you may drink." The voice said again, "If you are thirsty, come and drink."... The voice was not like a man's. It was deeper, wilder, and stronger; a sort of heavy, golden voice. It did not make her any less frightened than she had been before, but it made her frightened in rather a different way. "Are you not thirsty?" said the Lion. "I'm dying of thirst," said Jill. "Then drink," said the Lion. "May I—Could I— would you mind going away while I do?" said Jill. The lion answered this only by a look and a very low growl. And as Jill gazed at its motionless bulk, she realized that she might as well have asked the whole mountain to move aside for her convenience...."Will you promise not to—do anything to me, if I do come?" said Jill. "I make no promise," said the

Lion. Jill was so thirsty now that, without noticing it, she had come a step nearer. "Do you eat girls?" she said. "I have swallowed up girls and boys, men and women, kings and emperors, cities and realms", said the Lion. It didn't say this as if it were boasting, nor as if it were sorry, nor as if it were angry. It just said it. "I daren't come and drink," said Jill. "Then you will die of thirst," said the Lion. "Oh dear!" said Jill, coming another step nearer. "I suppose I must go and look for another stream then." "There is no other stream," said the Lion. It never occurred to Jill to disbelieve the Lion—no one who had seen his stern face could do that—and her mind suddenly made itself up. It was the worst thing she had ever had to do, but she went forward to the stream and knelt down, and began scooping up water in her hand. It was the coldest, most refreshing water she had ever tasted. You didn't need to drink much of it, for it quenched your thirst at once.

There is another important passage concerning Aslan in *The Horse and His Boy*. Two talking horses and a girl discuss the Lionhood of Aslan and whether this is to be believed in literally. The Lionhood is the Narnian equivalent of the personhood of God the Father and also of the human nature of God the Son: like any non-theist on our earth, Bree is the self-confident matter-of-fact horse who swears by the Lion, merely as a figure of speech, and is shocked that anyone should take Aslan to be a real lion. In his lecturer's voice, Bree explains condescendingly that "to speak of him as a Lion . . . only mean[s] he's as strong as a lion . . . it would be absurd and disrespectful to suppose he is a real Lion." Bree soon apologizes to Aslan when he is actually tickled in the ear by the Lion's whiskers, "Aslan . . . I'm afraid I must be rather a fool"—and this elicits the reply: "Happy the Horse who knows that while he is still young. Or the Human either." (I should add that I myself am uncomfortable with the response of the humbly believing mare Hwin which is, "Please . . . you're so beautiful. You may eat me if you like. I'd sooner be eaten by you than fed by anyone else.")

While the Lion is the pivotal symbol around which everything turns in all seven books, in the closing chapters of *The Last Battle* a stable in a field becomes the equivalent of the world beyond. Entering the stable is entering supernal life. To nonbelievers and to evil persons who enter it, it remains a small, dark and noisome place. To those who attain salvation, it contains a vast world for, in a mystic paradox, "its inside is greater than its outside." For them the inside not only contains the Real Narnia, but beyond and above that again, a further land of Narnian happiness. (Only one critic whom I have read has noticed this doubling of heavenly archetypes which, I confess, leaves me puzzled.)

It is just as we reach the apocalyptic description of the afterlife that the topic of non-Christian religions reappears. The Calormene religion has been condemned earlier as false and diabolic: Tash, its god, is a devil who has imposed himself as a god, and the Calormenes kill humans as sacrifices on his altar. Now we meet a good young Calormene, Emeth—the word is the Hebrew for *faithful* or true—who is saved because the worship he has been offering to Tash is totally pure and, without knowing it, is a seeking for Aslan. "Beloved," says Aslan, "unless thy desire has been for me thou wouldst not have sought so long and so truly. For all find what they truly seek." Concomitantly, an Aslan worshiper whose devotion takes evil forms will have performed no true devotion: "no service which is vile" says the Lion "can be done to me." So does this positive form of ecumenism countermand the negative one which I discussed earlier.[2]

There is before us now the business of testing Lewis's own critical writing to judge how his fantasies for children fitted into his model

---

[2] And, with a great deal of embarrassment, I shall go further. When Lewis was writing his Narnia books, he had recently had a student writing a B.Litt. thesis under him on 18th century English translations from Arabic. This no doubt led the conscientious supervisor to reread the *Arabian Nights*, the book of tales which has contributed so strongly to the background of *The Horse and His Boy*. The student himself came from that same background, but Lewis possibly noticed that he was attending

of the interrelationship between faith, literature and life in the world. Some impressions can be gained from his magazine article on writing for children, his book *An Experiment in Criticism* and a paper of his which, for reasons explained in it, is surrealistically called "Bluspells and Flalansferes." To sum up his views succinctly: imagination is as important an organ of investigation as reason is; as he writes, "Reason is the natural organ of truth; but imagination is the organ of meaning."

With imagination we create art and literature; especially, we create story and story transmits truth. The Lewis scholar Paul Ford writes: "Lewis saw the story as a bridge between two ways of knowing reality: thinking about it and experiencing it. Thinking is incurably abstract; experiencing is always concrete."

Fantasy, if used improperly, can become delusion or, as Lewis puts it, Morbid Castle-Building; to entertain it wrongly and incessantly is to injure oneself. But fantasy rightly used leads, at the least, to recreation through *normal* castle-building. But this too has its dangers, for you may dabble in it egoistically, making yourself the hero, giving yourself imaginary triumphs. Use it without this self-centeredness and you will obtain healthy recreation; pass further on, and it leads you to literary invention. This informs you of Truth, and will be found to be the ante-chamber that opens on to Faith. This happens through the writer's creating a subordinate world of his own: Lewis sees this as more conducive to truth than the program normally accepted by modern writers which is to create a "comment upon life."

So much for Lewis's own theoretical statements. Oddly enough, I believe we can learn more about the abstract underpinning of the Narnia stories by making a similar summing up of the ideas of another person, and that is his friend Tolkien. In 1946 Lewis put together a

---

the meetings which Lewis presided over, of the Socratic Club, a society for the rational discussion of the Christian religion. Perhaps he also noticed him at some of the public religious addresses that he gave. Just possibly, that is how, and in part only, of course, the character of Emeth took shape. And as you will by now have guessed, I am wondering if the flattering portrayal of Emeth is a Narnian transformation of myself.

collection of essays as a memorial volume for his friend Charles Williams: the essays were by different persons, all friends of the dead writer. One of the contributions was a long and weighty one by Tolkien with the title "On Fairy-Stories." It seems without doubt that Lewis was influenced by this essay both in his own expressed views on fantasy stories, and in the Narnia stories themselves.

In his essay Tolkien defends Fantasy by saying that it is not opposed to Reason; the keener the Reason, the better the Fantasy. Without the wish or the ability to see Truth, Fantasy languishes and turns into Morbid Delusion. There is no essential link between fairy tale and children; it is not true that children's credulity and their lack of experience make fairy tales suitable fare for them. It is true, however, that the child reader finds important the question of Right and Wrong.

It is also true that fairy tale shares elements with Myth. Humans are Subcreators and on to natural objects they imprint Personality. The fairy story has three faces. The Mystical Face looks towards the Supernatural. The Magical looks towards Nature. The one Tolkien calls the "Mirror of scorn and pity" looks towards Humanity. In writing Fantasy artists, as Subcreators, use their Will to make a Secondary World, and that world has its rules which things in it must follow. We make Fantasy in our measure "because we are made" and "made in the image and likeness of a Maker." The art produced by our imagination, if imagination is combined with Wonder, produces Fantasy.

Very debatably in my opinion, Tolkien seems to take all Fantasy to be a higher form than realism—does that mean that *The Hobbit is* a greater work than, say, Tolstoy's *War and Peace?* Fantasy may take different forms: strict and loose allegory are two forms; another is appreciative fantasy in which the secondary world is enjoyed for its own sake. Another is what has been called illustrative fantasy. This seems to be the form of the Narnia stories for, enjoyable though their world is for its own sake, in them a secondary world is used to make a point about the primary world.

Fantasy has three purposes. The first is Recovery: an experience of the Secondary World which restores us and refreshes our view of our

Primary World. This seems to be the factor which Lewis describes as Renewal, an *"excursion into the preposterous which strengthens our relish for real life."* The second factor is Escape: here Escape is used in a positive sense and not as we normally use the word "escapism." It is the Escape of a Prisoner, not the Flight of a Deserter. Escape satisfies desires unrealized in the Primary World. Third comes Consolation, described as an Escape from Death. It is the Consolation of the Happy Ending, the ending for which Tolkien makes up the word Eucatastrophe (from the Greek for *good* and for *turning away*). Tolkien in this sees a happy ending as an essential of the fairy tale; speaking of the Turn, as he calls those developments which lead up to the eucatastrophe, he says that it "reflects a glory backwards," giving a joy that transcends the event in the narrative.

It seems to me that Lewis in writing the last chapter of *The Last Battle* has done precisely that, giving fresh and transcending meaning to the human experience earlier in that book and in all the books that have gone before, and turning death in a railway accident, and defeat by an invading army, into freedom and happiness. Tolkien's own words, written some ten years before the final Narnia tale, succeed marvelously in encapsulating its meaning, pointing out both a theological and a literary importance. Theologically, they are a justification of the use of the Art of Comedy to convey spiritual truth. As literary criticism, they give to Comedy something of the deep and important status normally given only to Tragedy. Tolkien explains:

> It [Eucatastrophe] does not deny the existence of *dyscatastrophe*, of sorrow and failure: the possibility of these is necessary to the joy of deliverance; it denies (in the face of much evidence, if you will) universal final defeat and in so far is *evangelium*, giving a fleeting glimpse of Joy, Joy beyond the walls of the world, poignant as grief.

It is clear that Lewis's stress is upon the importance of imagination, even though his spokesperson the Professor, in speaking about Lucy's experience in *The Lion, The Witch and The Wardrobe*, suggests that logic is to be respected and is to be distinguished from "scientism." It is imagination which makes people more receptive to truth. Before they enter Narnia the children are thrilled at the environment in and around the Professor's house: they speculate about the rooms and corridors, the birds and animals and they explore the woods. They are prepared for the Narnian experience by Romantic pre-experience, which prepares one for truths greater than our own imaginings.

On the other hand, the threshold to the supernatural passes unrecognized by those who are imaginatively, and hence spiritually, closed. In *The Magician's Nephew* the witch Jadis doesn't realize the function and importance of the Wood between the Worlds, a sort of Black Hole by way of which one passes from one cosmos to another. Lewis writes: "I think her mind was of a sort which cannot remember that quiet place at all; however often you took her there and however long you left her there, she would still know nothing about it."

Even the spiritually open may in stubbornness refuse to acknowledge God's presence and guidance. Peter confesses to Aslan in *Prince Caspian* that he had in fact realized the Lion was close to him even when he was in denial: "I really believed it was him tonight. . . . I mean, deep down inside. Or I could have, if I'd let myself. But I just wanted to get out of the woods—and—oh, I don't know."

Some subjects, faced with spiritual reality, are unpersuadable, closed to actual experience. In the stable at the end of the world in *The Last Battle*, the unbelieving dwarfs see only dark where others see and smell flowers. When Lucy offers them some violets, they feel insulted for their impression is that she is "shoving a lot of filthy stable-litter in [their] face[s]."

I leave the last word to Aslan: "They will not let us help them. They have chosen *cunning* instead of *belief*. Their prison is only in their own minds, yet they are in that prison; and so afraid of being taken in that they cannot be taken out."

BIBLIOGRAPHY

A. Primary Sources

Hamilton, Clive (pseudonym for C.S. Lewis). *Dymer.* New York: E. P. Dutton, 1926.

. *Spirits in Bondage.* London: William Heinemann, 1919.

Lewis, C.S. *The Abolition of Man.* New York: Macmillan, 1947.

. *The Allegory of Love.* London: Oxford, 1936.

. *Arthurian Torso.* London: Oxford, 1948.

. "Awake My Lute," *Atlantic Monthly,* CLXXII (November, 1943), 113.

. *Beyond Personality.* New York: Macmillan, 1945.

. *The Case for Christianity.* New York: Macmillan, 1943.

. *Christian Behavior.* New York: Macmillan, 1943.

. "The Christian Hope—Its Meaning for Today," *Religion in Life,* XXI (1951), 20–32.

. *Christian Reflections.* Grand Rapids, Michigan: Eerdmans, 1967.

. "Donne and Love Poetry in the Seventeenth Century," *Seventeenth Century Studies Presented to Sir Herbert Grierson* (by several authors). Oxford: Clarendon, 1938.

. *English Literature in the Sixteenth Century.* Oxford: Clarendon, 1954.

. "Epitaph," *Spectator,* CLXXXI (July 30, 1948), 142.

. "Equality," *Spectator,* CLXXI (August 27, 1943), 192.

. "Evil and God," *Spectator,* CLXVI (February 7, 1941), 141.

. *George MacDonald.* New York: Macmillan, 1954.

. *The Great Divorce.* New York: Macmillan, 1946.

. *The Horse and His Boy.* New York: Macmillan, 1955.

. "Importance of an Ideal," *Living Age,* CCCLIX (October, 1940), 109–11.

. "Introduction" to D. E. Harding, *The Hierarchy of Heaven and Earth.* New York: Harper, 1952.

. "Introduction" to J.B. Phillips, *Letters to the Young Churches: A Translation of the New Testament Epistles.* New York: Macmillan, 1940.

. *The Last Battle.* London: The Bodley Head, 1956.

. *Letters of C.S. Lewis.* Edited and with a memoir by W.H. Lewis. San Diego: Harcourt, Brace & World, 1966.

. *Letters to Children*. Edited by Lyle Dorsett and Marjorie Lamp Mead. New York: Macmillan, 1985.
. "Lilies That Fester," *Twentieth Century*, CLXVII (April, 1955), 330–41.
. *The Lion, the Witch and the Wardrobe*. New York: Macmillan, 1950.
. *The Literary Impact of the Authorized Version*. London: University of London, Athlone Press, 1950.
. *The Magician's Nephew*. New York: Macmillan, 1955.
. "March for Drum, Trumpet, and Twenty-one Giants," *Punch*, CCXXV (November 4, 1953), 553.
. *Mere Christianity*. New York: Macmillan,
. *Miracles*. New York: Macmillan, 1947.
. "On a Picture by Chirico," *Spectator*, CLXXXII (May 6, 1954), 607.
. *Out of the Silent Planet*. New York: Macmillan, 1943.
. "The Pains of Animals," *Atlantic Monthly*, CLXXXVI (August, 1950), 559–61.
. *Perelandra*. New York: Macmillan, 1952.
. *The Personal Heresy*. London: Oxford, 1939.
. *The Pilgrim's Regress*. New York: Sheed and Ward, 1944.
. "Preface" to B. G. Sandhurst, *How Heathen is Britain?* London: Collins, 1947.
. "Preface" and "On Stories," *Essays Presented to Charles Williams* (compiled by C.S. Lewis). London: Oxford, 1947. (Available in paperback edition. Grand Rapids, Michigan: Wm. B. Eerdmans, 1966).
. *A Preface to Paradise Lost*. London: Oxford University Press, 1942.
. *Prince Caspian*. New York: Macmillan, 1951.
. "Private Bates," *Spectator*, CLXXIII (December, 1944), 496.
. *The Problem of Pain*. New York: Macmillan, 1948.
. "Psychoanalysis and Literary Criticism," *Essays and Studies*, XXVII (1942), 21.
. *Rehabilitations and Other Essays*. London: Oxford, 1939.
. "The Salamander," *Spectator*, CLXXIV (June 8, 1945), 521.
. *The Screwtape Letters*. New York: Macmillan, 1943.
. "The Shoddy Lands," *The Best from Fantasy and Science Fiction. Sixth Series* (edited by Anthony Boucher). New York: Doubleday and Company, 1957.
. *The Silver Chair*. New York: Macmillan, 1953.
. *Surprised by Joy*. London: Geoffrey Bles, 1955.

. *That Hideous Strength.* New York: Macmillan, 1946.

. *Till We Have Faces.* London: Geoffrey Bles, 1956.

. "To G. M.," *Spectator,* CLXIX (October 9, 1942), 335.

. "Under Sentence," *Spectator,* CLXXVI (September 7, 1945), 219.

. *The Voyage of the "Dawn Treader."* New York: Macmillan, 1952.

. *The Weight of Glory and Other Addresses.* New York: Macmillan, 1949.

. "The World's Last Night," *His,* XV (May, 1955), 1–4, 22–24.

B. Secondary Sources

Andersen, Hans Christian. *Fairy Tales.* New York: Garden City, 1932.

Anderson, George C. "C.S. Lewis: Foe of Humanism," *Christian Century,* LXIII (December 25, 1946), 1562–63.

Auden, W. H. "Red Lizards and White Stallions," *The Saturday Review of Literature, XXIX* (April 13, 1946), 22.

Augustinus, Aurelius. *The Confessions of St. Augustine.* New York: Pocket Books, 1953.

Bacon, Leonard. "The Imaginative Power of C.S. Lewis," *The Saturday Review of Literature,* XXVII (April 8, 1944), 9.

Brady, Charles A. "Introduction to Lewis," *America,* (May 27, 1944), pp. 213–14; (June 10, 1944), pp. 269–70.

Brown, Katharine L. "An 'Exquisitely Beautiful' Hymn," *The Living Church,* (April 2, 1995), 12, 15.

Bunyan, John. *The Pilgrim's Progress.* Charlotte, North Carolina: Books for Christians, 1972.

Chesterton, G.K. *William Blake.* London: Duckworth, 1910.

Cooke, Alistair. "Mr. Anthony at Oxford," *New Republic,* CX (April 24, 1944), 578–80.

Dickens, Charles. *Martin Chuzzlewit.* London: Dent, 1907.

Driberg, Tom. "Lobbies of the Soul," *New Statesman,* XLIX (March 19, 1955), 393.

Empson, William. *Some Versions of Pastoral.* Norfolk, Connecticut: James Laughlin, New Directions, 1935.

Friar, Kimon, and John Malcolm Brinnin. *Modern Poetry.* New York: Appleton-Century-Crofts, 1951.

Gilbert, Alan H. "Critics of Mr. C.S. Lewis on Milton's Satan," *South Atlantic Quarterly*, XLVII (April, 1948), 216–25.

Grahame, Kenneth. *The Wind in the Willows*. New York: Scribner's, 1954.

Green, Roger Lancelyn and Walter Hooper. *C.S. Lewis: A Biography*. London: Collins, 1974.

Grennan, Margaret R. "The Lewis Trilogy: A Scholar's Holiday," *Catholic World*, CLXVII (July, 1948), 337–44.

Haldane, J.B.S. "God and Mr. C.S. Lewis," *The Rationalist Annual*. London: Watts, 1948.

Hamilton, Edith. *Mythology*. New York: The New American Library of World Literature, 1953.

Hamm, Victor M. "Mr. Lewis in Perelandra," *Thought: Fordham University Quarterly*, XX (June, 1945), 271–90.

Harrison, Charles T. "The Renaissance Epitomized," *Sewanee Review*, LXIII (Winter, 1955), 153–61.

Hoffman, James W. "A Christian in Spite of Himself," *Presbyterian Life*, IX (February 4, 1956), 10–11, 28.

Joad, C.E.M. "Mr. Lewis's Devil," *The New Statesman and Nation*, XXIII (May 16, 1942), 324.

Kelly, Thomas R. *A Testament of Devotion*. New York: Harper, 1941.

Lee, E. George. *C.S. Lewis and Some Modern Theologians*. London: The Lindsey Press, 1944.

MacDonald, George. *The Princess and the Goblin*. New York: Macmillan, 1926.

———. *The Princess and Curdie*. London: Penguin Books, 1966.

"The Man on the Cover," *Pulpit Digest*, XXXVI (March, 1956), 22.

Myres, John L. "Miracles," *Nature*, CLX (August 30, 1947), 275–76.

Nesbit, Edith. *The Magic World*. London: Ernest Benn Limited, 1959.

Phillips, J.B. *Your God Is Too Small*. New York: Macmillan, 1955.

"The Reluctant Convert," *Time*, LXVII (February 6, 1956), 98.

Sayer, George. *Jack: A Life of C.S. Lewis*. Wheaton, Illinois: Crossway Books, 1994.

Sayers, Dorothy. *The Mind of the Maker*. New York: Harcourt, Brace, 1941.

Soper, David Wesley. "Dorothy Sayers and the Christian Synthesis," *Religion in Life*, XXI (1951), 21.

Thompson, Francis. *The Hound of Heaven.* Mount Vernon, New York Peter Pauper.

Thompson, Stith. *The Folktale.* New York: Dryden, 1946.

"Time Disciplined," *Times Literary Supplement,* No. 2773 (March 25, 1955), 181.

Tolkien, J.R.R. "On Fairy Stories," *Essays Presented to Charles Williams* (compiled by C.S. Lewis). London: Oxford, 1947.

Wagner, Richard. *The Ring of the Nibelung* (translated by Margaret Armour). New York: Garden City, 1939.

Wain, John. "Pleasure, Controversy, and Scholarship," *The Spectator,* CXCI-II (October 1, 1954), 403.

Walsh, Chad. "Back to Faith," *The Saturday Review of Literature,* XXXIX (March 3, 1956), 32.

. "C.S. Lewis and the Christian Life," *Catholic World,* CLXVIII (February, 1949), 370–75.

. "C.S. Lewis, Apostle to the Skeptics." *Atlantic Monthly,* CLXXVIII (September 1946), 115–19.

. *C.S. Lewis, Apostle to Skeptics.* New York: Macmillan, 1949.

. "The Pros and Cons of C.S. Lewis," *Religion in Life,* XVIII (1949), 222–28.

Williams, Charles, ed. *The Letters of Evelyn Underhill.* London: Longmans, Green, 1943.

. *The Place of the Lion.* New York: Pellegrini and Cudahy, 1951.

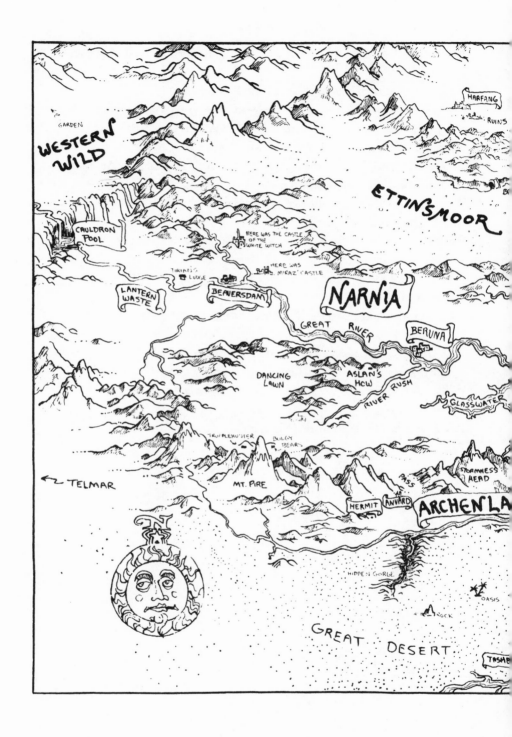

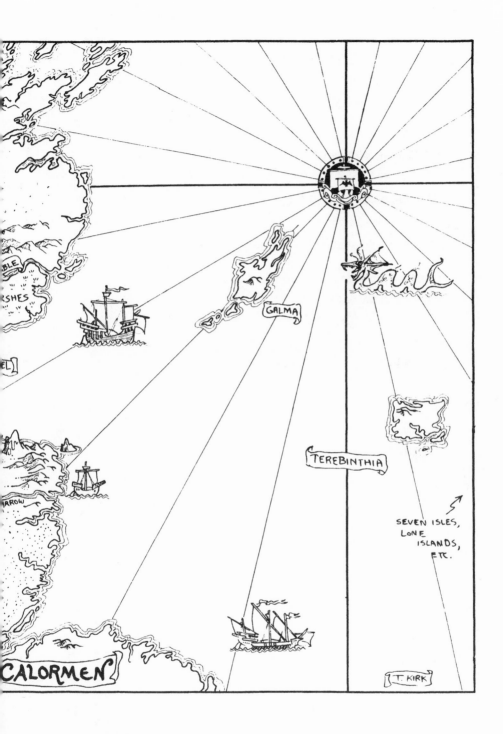

CALORMEN

GALMA

TEREBINTHIA

SEVEN ISLES,
LONE
ISLANDS,
ETC.

T. KIRK

Additional copies of this book may be obtained from your local bookstore, or by sending $18.95 per paperback copy postpaid to:

Hope Publishing House
P.O. Box 60008
Pasadena, CA 91116

California residents please add 8¼% sales tax
Fax orders to: 626-792-2121
Telephone VISA/MC orders to: 800-326-2671
E-mail
Web si